Just '50s

MEMORABLE MACHINES FROM AMERICA'S FAVORITE DECADE

Copyright ©2010 F+W Media, Inc.

All rights reserved. No portion of this publication may be reproduced or transmitted in any form or by any means, electronic or mechanical, including photocopy, recording, or any information storage and retrieval system, without permission in writing from the publisher, except by a reviewer who may quote brief passages in a critical article or review to be printed in a magazine or newspaper, or electronically transmitted on radio, television, or the Internet.

Published by

Krause Publications, a division of F+W Media, Inc.
700 East State Street • Iola, WI 54990-0001
715-445-2214 • 888-457-2873
www.krausebooks.com

To order books or other products call toll-free 1-800-258-0929
or visit us online at www.krausebooks.com or www.Shop.Collect.com

Library of Congress Control Number: 2010925546

ISBN-13: 978-1-4402-1426-4
ISBN-10: 1-4402-1426-3

Designed by Sharon Bartsch
Edited by Angelo Van Bogart and Brian Earnest

Printed in the United States of America

CONTENTS

FOREWORD 4
CHAPTER 1 1950 Olds Rocket Eight 5
CHAPTER 2 1950s Hudson Hornets 10
CHAPTER 3 1950 Tailfins 17
CHAPTER 4 1952-'54 Nash-Healey 23
CHAPTER 5 1952 Mercury 26
CHAPTER 6 1953 Buick Skylark 28
CHAPTER 7 1953-'54 Kaiser-Darrin 31
CHAPTER 8 1953-'54 Plymouth 34
CHAPTER 9 1954 Dodge Royal 500 38
CHAPTER 10 1954 Ford Crestline 41
CHAPTER 11 1954 Mercury XM-800 43
CHAPTER 12 1954 Chevrolet Nomad 48
CHAPTER 13 1955 Chicago Auto Show 53
CHAPTER 14 1955 Mercury 61
CHAPTER 15 1955-'56 Chrysler 300 65
CHAPTER 16 1956 Metropolitan 70
CHAPTER 17 1956 Studebaker Truck 75
CHAPTER 18 1956-'57 El Morocco 77
CHAPTER 19 1956-'57 Lincolns 81
CHAPTER 20 1957 Chevrolet Bel Air 86
CHAPTER 21 1957 Nash 89
CHAPTER 22 1957 Plymouth 92
CHAPTER 23 1957 Plymouth Tulsarama! Aftermath 97
CHAPTER 24 1957 Pontiac 101
CHAPTER 25 Ford's 1957-'59 Ford Retractable 105
CHAPTER 26 1958 Buick 111
CHAPTER 27 1958-'60 Edsel 115
CHAPTER 28 1958 Fargo Trucks 118
CHAPTER 29 1958 Studebaker Hawk 121
CHAPTER 30 1959 Cadillac Fleetwood Sixty Special 124
CHAPTER 31 1959 De Soto At Daytona 127
CHAPTER 32 1959 General Motors 133

FOREWORD

CRUISING BACK IN TIME!

The 1950s. It was an unforgettable time in American history. Rock music dawned, segregation ended, and wide-screen movies debuted. Duck tails, saddle shoes, and hula-hoops were all the rage.

And those fabulous 1950s cars! Big and roomy, with lots of glass and chrome, with new styles every year. They sported fabulous fins and ever-growing V-8s under the hood. Chevrolet, Ford and Chrysler competed with Hudson, Nash and Studebaker for business.

Whether you lived through the 1950s, or just wonder what those great years were like — and what those great cars were like when they were new — "*Just '50s*" is for you.

Travel back more than five decades and revisit some of the great cars of the era that never seems to grow old.

CHAPTER 1 | **1950 OLDS ROCKET EIGHT**

By Linda Clark

OLDS ROCKET 88s
'50s Futuramic fliers

On May 30, 1949, the new Rocket 88 was seen by more than 200,000 racing fans when it paced the Indianapolis 500. Later, one of the special pace cars graced a dealer's showroom. Note the special rocket emblems on the pace car's front fender and door.

Oldsmobile nearly wobbled the world on its axis with its Rocket V-8 in 1949. You can't say Olds invented the hot rod in America, but at a time when Detroit was just about getting the olive drab flushed out of the spray guns, this feisty V-8, encased in a Futuramic body, booted the family car onto a whole new level of gut-punching performance.

The 88's lumpy styling and 135 horses may seem feeble by today's standards, but among the portholed Buicks of the day, it was dynamite. The Rocket 88 introduced a generation of kids to the speeding ticket and turned formerly staid grown-ups into wild-eyed road hunters.

The funniest part was, it was by accident. Or maybe Olds general manager Sherrod Skinner and his Rocket engineering team of Gil Burrell, Jack Wolfram, Harold Metzel

The 1950 Olds 88 had the same mechanicals as the '49, but had restyled front bumper guards, a new front fender trim piece and distinctive V-8 Rocket hood ornament for the first time.

and Lowell Kintigh made it look that way. They boasted only of "The New Thrill" of Futuramic styling. But they no doubt knew the Rocket 88's potential, as did hot-rodders.

A V-8 was not new in 1949, nor was it in Lansing. Oldsmobile had one as early as 1915, and in 1929, the automaker built the L-head Viking V-8 with horizontally located valves. Although a sales failure, the Viking eventually led both Olds and Cadillac to prominence in the overhead-valve V-8 field. It was Cadillac that developed the modern-day V-8 first, but Olds took no backseat when it came to putting the high-performance V-8 into production. Sherrod Skinner foresaw the wisdom of putting the potent new powerplant into a compact, lightweight body. Thus was launched the beginning of the postwar horsepower race.

Immediately after World War II, Cadillac was moving swiftly toward a wide-bore, short-stroke, oversquare design with slippered pistons and a short, stiff, five-main-bearing crankshaft. Initially dictated by the period's technology and the development of high-octane fuels during the war, this design finally crystallized for both Cadillac and Olds with the experiments of GM's research giant, Charles Kettering.

Oldsmobile's 88s stirred interest with the public, as well as competing manufacturers. This photo of a 1949 88 sedan is from the archives of Kaiser-Frazer (note the Frazer in the background).

The Olds folks looked more to Kettering's experiments with high-compression, short-stroke and stiff-crank engines than they ever did to Cadillac. Kettering's research had, in effect, opened their eyes to the high-compression potential for economy and performance. Olds engineers found the existing L-head design had a compression ratio of 8.0 to 1. Beyond that, it ran roughly and noisily, caused by a lack of crankshaft rigidity, which dictated a short, rigid crank in any new engine. Cadillac developed an oversquare design and slippered pistons, but Oldsmobile developed the rest of the Rocket V-8 independent of Cadillac.

Initially, the engine displaced 287 cubic inches (later 303.7). During its development, it was referred to as the Kettering Engine. But to set it apart from Cadillac's overhead-valve V-8, it was later dubbed the "Rocket" by Oldsmobile. Thought by some to be too much engine for a small car, the Rocket V-8 was originally intended for use only in the largest Oldsmobiles.

Engine production began on Nov. 3, 1948, and although the Rocket V-8's valve diameters were the same as the Cadillac V-8, there were no interchangeable parts in the two engines. With its 7.25-to-1 compression ratio, the Rocket engine developed

In 1952, Oldsmobile's bread and butter was the 88 sedan — a car that packed punch, and the family on the way to a picnic.

135 hp at 3,600 rpm. When Cadillac learned the Olds engine would displace 303.7 cubic inches, it raised the size of its own V-8 from 309 to 331 cubic inches.

The 88 appeared in February 1949, and by the end of the year, 99,276 cars had been built. There were 10 models in all, but the Standard and Deluxe four-door sedans were the best sellers. There were only 5,434 convertibles built and 11,561 88 Club Coupes in Standard and Deluxe form. Although Olds had pioneered the Rocket V-8's mechanics, it had nothing to do with the basic body design, which was GM's 1949 A-body shared with Pontiac and Chevrolet. Olds gave the car "Futuramic" identity patterned after the trim of the larger 98, whose styling, like Cadillac's, was inspired by Harley Earl.

The 88's styling wasn't unique, but Olds had its own X frame and suspension. The 88 also weighed 300 pounds less than the 98. On May 30, 1949, a new Rocket 88 was seen by more than 200,000 race fans as it paced the Indianapolis 500. By then, the 88 was known as the hottest car in America. That same year, Bill France created a late-model stock car division for the then-infant NASCAR. Olds dominated that first Grand National season, with Red Baron taking the championship and Bob Flock placing second, both in 88s. Olds ended up winning six of the year's nine events.

It hardly mattered that there were no high-performance options for the 88 in 1949, because there was little to do to the car. The Rocket V-8 was so successful, in fact, that the six-cylinder series was dropped in mid 1950. During 1950, Olds was again NASCAR champ with 10 victories in 19 races entered. Europeans were also impressed with the Olds 88's triumph in a Spa-Francorchamps race for production cars, in which an Olds 88 won again in 1952 and 1953. In May 1950, Herschel McGriff and Ray Elliott won the first of the famous Mexican Road Races with a 1950 Olds 88 notchback two-door sedan.

The 1950 model differed stylistically from the '49. Both cars were the same mechanically, but for 1950, the front bumper guards were restyled, and the hood sported a distinctive V-8 Rocket ornament for the first time. A long front fender trim piece was added, and the "88" on the front fender and the Futuramic plate on the lower side trim piece were eliminated. The rear fender mudguard was brought forward and carried the word "Futuramic." The taillight fins bore "88" imprints and Olds' famous World Ring, which appeared in front in 1949, was placed on the rear deck in 1950 as a trunk handle. The rear deck also sported a "Rocket 88" emblem. Dashboards for both years were the same — a half-moon instrument cluster that dated back to the 1938 model. Olds began offering high-performance options, too, in 1950, as a so-called "export kit" for the 88. The 88's 119.5-inch wheelbase remained unchanged for 1950.

In 1951, Olds introduced a Super 88 with an all-new body on a 120-inch wheelbase that boasted a one-piece windshield and a three-piece wraparound rear window. Olds continued to dominate NASCAR through 1951, capturing 20 wins in 41 races. In 1952, the Super 88's horsepower was boosted from 135 to 160, and greater breathing capacity was provided by a new Rochester Quadrajet carburetor, which Olds shared with Buick and Cadillac. Olds finished the 1952 NASCAR season with only nine victories, trailing Hudson.

Despite track difficulties, Super 88 sales were 333,464 in 1953, with engines now reaching 165 horsepower and Olds offering a new 12-volt electrical system, power brakes and optional air conditioning. Although an Olds 88 set a new two-way average (113.38 mph) at the 1954 Daytona Speed Weeks, Hudson Hornets now dominated the Grand National circuit. Racing had little influence on sales, however, and 1954 was a good year for Lansing.

So who cares that Olds never intended for the Rocket 88 to be the hottest car in America? That was before history took over.

| CHAPTER 2 | 1950s HUDSON HORNETS |

By Phil Hall

STUNG BY HORNETS
Marshall Teague and some high-powered Hudsons were a nearly unbeatable team

After the Aug. 23, 1953, 100-mile AAA race at Wisconsin State Fair Park Speedway, the top two finishers pulled up to the finish line. Sam Hanks drove the #71 Hornet to victory over Marshall Teague's Fabulous Hudson Hornet #1. Both drivers were just getting out of their cars.

One of the legends of early late-model stock car racing is that of the Hudson Hornet. In a world of emerging overhead-valve V-8 power, the L-head Hornet six dominated the sport — at least for a few years.

It was the threat of the new V-8s that prompted the Hudson Motor Car Co. to boost its 262-cid six to 308 cubes for 1951 and put it in its largest (124-inch wheelbase) models with the new name Hudson Hornet. This was the answer to the Oldsmobile 88, new Chrysler FirePower Hemi V-8 and, to a lesser extent, the Cadillac and new Studebaker V-8s.

The vehicle package was not a new one, as Hudson opened the 1951 model year

Marshall Teague's "Fabulous" Hudson Hornet took AAA stock cars by storm in 1952. Here, he is shown on his way to victory in the July 13 150-miler (above). Back when stock cars had doors, Marshall Teague posed with his Hornet before the start of the 100-mile race on Aug. 23, 1953 (below). Teague finished second that day. Behind him is the Hornet of Johnny Mantz.

with its "step-down" unitized body, which first saw light in the 1948 models.

Racing was not even remotely part of the plan for the new Hornet. That component came from Marshall Teague, owner of Gateway Service in Daytona Beach, Fla. Teague, who started racing locally in 1945, tried to race Hudsons off and on, but without much success. When the 1951 Hornet came along, he immediately saw the advantage of the torque-rich big 308-cid H-145 six and the fine-handling Hudson chassis,

with its low center of gravity, center-point steering and "crab-leg" tread with the front wider than the rear.

He entered the new Hornet in the Feb. 11 Daytona Beach NASCAR 160-mile Grand National on the beach/road course and scored a convincing victory, the first for Hudson in NASCAR's stock car division. Teague rubbed it in the competition's nose by lettering his mount the "Fabulous Hudson Hornet."

There are a couple of versions of the

Jack McGrath won the pole for the Aug. 23, 1953, AAA 100-miler in his 1953 Hornet. Before the start of the race, he checked the air pressure while crewmen look under the hood in this photo. Note the full chrome trim and license plate.

story, but he made his way to Detroit to talk with Hudson engineers about ways to improve the Hornet for racing. At first, the engineers didn't know who he was or that their Hornets were being raced but, eventually, Teague made a connection, and the flow of heavy-duty parts that would help his cars stay together made the parts list and became legal for use in racing.

Included was Twin-H induction with two single-barrel carburetors, which first became an over-the-counter parts kit and later a production offering. The design dated back to about 1944, and had been sitting on the shelves at Hudson.

Teague's victory was not unnoticed. At Daytona, there was only one other Hudson in the race. As the season progressed, Hudsons were entered in increasing numbers, and by season's end, a dozen events were won by Hornets (with Teague taking five). Oldsmobile's 20 topped the tally.

In the course of the season, Teague added Plymouth driver Herb Thomas to his team

Driving a recently repaired backup 1953 Hudson, Sam Hanks went on to win the Aug. 23, 1953, 100-mile AAA race. He is shown passing Cecil Hayes' 1953 Packard

and supplied Hudsons, also labeled "Fabulous." Thomas won the season championship for 1951.

However, all was not going well for Teague in "NASCAR Land." His points were taken away for running in non-sanctioned events, including the Carrera Panamericana (Mexican Road Race) where he finished sixth. He had to pay a fine to be reinstated for the 1952 Daytona event, which he again won. Thomas placed second, for a 1-2 Hudson finish.

As it turned out, 1952 would be a banner year for Hudson drivers, who scored 27 wins out of the 34 Grand Nationals.

However, Teague was only a minor factor with two wins, as yet another dispute with NASCAR over non-sanctioned races resulted in him leaving the circuit after the March 30 event at North Wilkesboro, N.C. Despite the distance, Teague joined the stock car circuit of the American Automobile Association (AAA) Contest Board, which had a far smaller schedule and ran primarily in the Midwest.

A feature of the AAA stock cars was the attraction of Indy Car drivers racing stocks when schedules permitted. AAA stock cars had only three events during the 1951 season, all on the mile at Milwaukee. To get more dates, they added half-miles to the schedule for 1952, which gave them 13 events.

A few Hudson Hornets ran AAA in 1951, but without success. All that changed when Teague brought his Fabulous Hudson

Hudsons were rapidly eclipsed in AAA stock car racing in 1955. Here, Dick Houdek's 1954 Hornet (#11) gets passed by a Chrysler C-300.

Hornet to AAA on May 11 at Toledo, Ohio. He won the contest on the half-mile and the next four events on the schedule, as well.

Teague won two more AAA races that year, and fellow Hudson drivers Jack McGrath (3), Frank Luptow (2) and Frank Mundy joined in to give Hudsons 12-straight wins on the 13-event schedule. The lone win for the competition was in the opener at Pomona, Calif., on Feb. 24 when Jim Rigsby bested the field in an Oldsmobile. Teague was the 1952 champion with 1,980 points to 980 for runner-up Luptow.

It was often mentioned that Teague joined AAA to be able to run in the Indianapolis 500. That may have been secondary to his dislike of NASCAR. He did compete in two Indy 500s, in 1953 and '57, and select other Indy Car events. In the 1953 Indy 500, he finished 18th. His best was '57, when he drove the Sumar Special to seventh place.

Ironically, Teague was killed on Feb. 11, 1959, while testing for a proposed Indy Car race at the brand-new Daytona International Speedway. He was driving the much-modified Sumar Special, which flipped over at the NASCAR track. Despite his dislike of NASCAR, Teague did want to run in an Indy Car event at Daytona.

Listed on the 1953 schedule were 17 AAA stock car contests. Hudsons won 14 of them, leaving two to Packard driver Don O'Dell and one for Olds. Frank Mundy of Atlanta, Ga., scored five wins and took the championship. O'Dell finished second, Nash driver Bob Christie wound up third

With a 1954 Hudson Hornet pace car and Marshall Teague's new Hudson on the pole, the Sept. 12 200-miler turned out to be the last hurrah at the track for the make. Teague won and with it the season AAA stock car championship.

and Teague, who broke his tradition with the number six and carried the number one, placed fourth. Teague scored three wins in 1953, as did fifth-place Jack McGrath. Indy star Sam Hanks also scored a pair of Hudson wins.

Helping the Hudson cause in AAA and NASCAR for 1953 was the 7X engine. Billed as an over-the-parts-counter powerplant for police and high-altitude driving, it was just what the racers needed, as competition was getting stiffer that season. Blocks were slightly overbored and stress relieved and had a reworked 232 head for higher compression, plus a high-lift cam, larger valves, split exhaust manifold and other features. It was announced in August 1953, but racers had them in service well before that. No official horsepower was released, but estimates put the 7X around the 220 mark.

For the 1954 AAA season, Hudson should have had a rough time, as a new 235-hp Chrysler New Yorker Deluxe and powerful Buick Century had the potential to out-muscle it. However, AAA (and NASCAR) decided to crack down on all the speed equipment that was being listed for some brands. This stricter interpretation favored the Hudsons, which, at this point, were closer to stock than most of the competitors.

Early-season West Coast events gave Hudson three initial 1954 wins, one of them

On lap 43 of the 1953 AAA 100-miler, McGrath was involved in a crash and flipped the car three times. He received a minor wrist injury, but the car was totaled, as seen behind the wrecker. He was credited with 32nd place out of the 36 starters.

by Teague March 28 at Phoenix, Ariz.

When the series arrived at its big track, the newly paved Milwaukee Mile, Chryslers entered by Carl Kiekhaefer held sway. Tony Bettenhausen won the July 11 150-miler in a Chrysler, and Frank Mundy came aboard from Hudson to take two races at the track in August for Chrysler. One of them, on Aug. 22, is wrongly listed in AAA records as a Hudson win.

Teague held his ground and collected his fifth win of the 1954 season in the last event on the schedule, a 200-miler at Milwaukee on Sept. 12. It was his last win in a Hudson and the last Hudson win in AAA stock history. Teague ran all 16 events on the 1954 schedule and claimed his second and final AAA title, 2,320 points to 1,320 for Sam Hanks, who started nine contests.

Hudson Motor Car Co. became part of American Motors in 1954, and production of the step-downs ended in October of that year. The 1955 Hudson was based on the Nash and had no potential, nor backing, as a race car.

For 1955, a few Hudsons plied the AAA schedule, but the Kiekhaefer Chrysler 300s ruled the series, taking 10 wins in 13 events. Teague switched to Chevrolet and had some success. He raced them into 1957. AAA was replaced by the United States Auto Club (USAC) starting in 1956. A similar eclipse happened in NASCAR, with the 79th and final Hudson win early in 1955.

Editor's note: Photos from author's collection and taken at Wisconsin State Park Speedway near Milwaukee, Wis.

CHAPTER 3 / **1950 TAILFINS**

By John L. Gann, Jr.

FABULOUS FINS OF THE '50s

More than just for looks, fins reduced need for steering overcorrections

Tailfins became both a symbol of the 1950s and part of American popular culture, as this '57 Plymouth Fury on display at the Michigan State Museum in Lansing suggests.

It's probably the ultimate visual symbol of the "Fabulous '50s," not just for car people, but for everyone else, as well. It went from being part of our cars to becoming part of our culture.

It's said to have originated in 1948 with Cadillac, the car billed as "The Standard of the World." And it reached an apogee some would characterize as excess with the same marque exactly 11 years later before falling into rapid decline.

It's the tailfin

Aircraft were arguably the dominant influence on postwar American cars. We had "rocket" engines, "jet smooth" rides, propeller-nosed Fords and Studebakers, Strato-Streak Pontiacs and jet exhaust-inspired tail

In the 1950s, it was hard to top "The Standard of the World," and that was certainly true in the tail fin department, as this '59 Cadillac proves.

ends. Most new-car-buying households were, after all, headed by returned World War II servicemen, many of whom had their first real exposure to planes during the conflict.

But most prominent among the various aviation-inspired features were tall vertical projections above both rear fenders: tailfins.

Chrysler's "Forward Look"

The fin is commonly traced to the 1948 Cadillac, which had tiny humps housing taillamps at the ends of otherwise conventional rear fenders. They continued for eight years as an almost entirely unimitated trademark (though their reflection appeared in the upturned tails of the 1951 Henry J and 1952 Aero Willys). But what really got fins going were the mid-decade offerings from the Chrysler Corp.

In styling at least, MoPar vehicles of the early 1950s were the sensible shoes of the American car world. Conservatively styled and tall enough to support hat-wearing passengers under Chrysler President K.T. Keller, they lacked appeal for many buyers. But Chrysler did a 180-degree turn in 1955, introducing styling chief Virgil Exner's "Forward Look" on its entire line.

But these lower, sleeker "look of motion" bodies with wraparound windshields were not unique, since Ford introduced new models with much the same characteristics the same year, and Buick, Olds and Cadillac had brought out similar models the year before.

What set Chrysler apart was a facelift of the 1955 bodies the next year that topped the rear fenders of all its cars with blade-like fins. In contrast, the minimally facelifted 1956 bodies from Ford and GM looked as fresh as yesterday's newspaper.

Rocking their world in 1957

What made the fins of the '56 Chrysler cars more important than those of the '48 Cadillac was that they were copied.

The "New Kind of Ford" in 1957 added tiny fins, even to the Thunderbird. Lincoln went all the way with sizeable rear blades taken from the 1955 *Futura* dream car. That same year, the Studebaker Hawk grew its first fins, and the classic '57 Chevy extended blade-like fenders back, but not above the previous fender line. Even Cadillac's upturned fender ends became more Chrysler-like for 1957.

But in the words of advertising for the '58 Plymouth, there was "no catching the leader." While its competitors were just beginning to achieve parity with its 1956 move, Chrysler rocked the automotive world with an all-new line in 1957.

Wide, ultra-low bodies with slender roofs, low beltlines and vast glass areas departed from anything the factory had previously produced. And fins were more prominent than ever, extending far above the beltline and becoming a defining element in a dart-like or wedge-shaped body design rather than mere add-on fender ornamentation.

"Suddenly," boasted the 1957 Plymouth ads with little exaggeration, "it's 1960." The factory had completed the transition from sensible to sexy.

New forms for fins

GM's 50th-anniversary bodies in 1958 were more handsome than ever, but looked dated against their Chrysler rivals, as did Ford's offerings. But the king of the automotive hill wasn't about to be bested by a third-ranked contender. So GM scrapped the '58 bodies in 1959 in a move that gave Chevy and Pontiac three completely different bodies in as many years. The entire 1959 GM line was lower and wider than ever and even glassier than the Mopar competition. And every model sported tailfins.

Thanks in part to tapering rear quarter panels, the '59 Cadillac's upright fins appeared to top anything from Chrysler in height, and they have today become the stereotypical tailfins of the 1950s. But GM was more imaginative in the rest of its line.

Dramatic body sculpturing created large canted "Delta-wing" fins in the Buick and a gull-wing variation on Chevrolet, yet neither rose above the beltline as on the Chrysler products. More modest rocket-trail tubular projections – themselves topped by minuscule blade-like chrome fins – gave the Oldsmobile a sort of fin-on-fin look. But perhaps the fins with the most finesse were the tiny dual-canted sproutings atop backup lamps on the first of the "Wide Track" Pontiacs.

Horizontal fins similar to, but much small-

Fins with finesse. Pontiac signed on to the tail fin trend for just a single year, with modest diverging twins on each fender in 1959.

er and more conservative than those on Chevrolet, appeared on the all-new 1960 Ford, replacing tubular fender toppings in the also new, but conservatively styled, '59 models. Before dropping fins on its downsized 1962 line, Dodge also got creative. Its 1961 models featured handsome backward fins that began at the tail end of the car and grew higher before ending at the C-pillar. Some concept cars of the era showed a single fin over the rear deck instead of two atop fenders.

The engineering rationale

Were fins anything more than a sometimes outlandish automotive fashion? Chrysler, their popularizer — if not also their true originator — insisted they were.

The "real beauty" of "stabilizer" tailfins, according to the sales brochure for the 1960 Plymouth, "is in the engineering behind them. Wind tunnel tests at the University of Detroit show that these stabilizers reduce by 20 percent the steering corrections that you would normally make in a cross wind." The factory added that fins also cut 25 percent of the steering effort made necessary by cross winds.

The fins, it was explained, served to move the car's center of pressure further to the rear. "We try not to overlook anything," the brochure assured the buyer, "that will make Plymouth easy to handle." With Chrysler in its fifth year of finned vehicles, there may have been a touch of defensiveness in the explanation. It was to little avail, however, since in a major facelift of the 1960 body,

Tail fins weren't always vertical, and Ford followed Chevrolet in 1960 with wing-like appendages on an all-new body.

the 1961 Plymouth appeared with no fins at all, the laws of physics being apparently no match for the laws of fashion.

The Finis of the Fin

The Anglo-Saxon origin of our own word means "wing" or "feather." In Spanish and French, however, the word "fin" means "end." And engineering claims aside, by 1960 Chrysler was swimming against the tide. The end was indeed near.

That same year Chevrolet, Buick, and Cadillac trimmed their fins and Pontiac and Olds dropped theirs altogether. Most significantly, among the newest cars from Detroit in 1960 – the compact Corvair, Falcon, and Valiant – none sported tailfins unless you count the stubby projections at the tail end of the retro-styled Valiant. The Mercury Comet variation on the Falcon body was, however, outfitted with prominent fins, perhaps only to distinguish it from the very similar Ford.

In 1961 fins were absent from the entire GM line save Cadillac. They survived on the beautifully restyled '61 Thunderbird. But none of the rest of the Chrysler line followed Plymouth's finlessness until 1962. Rambler and the Studebaker Hawk also shed their fins in 1962.

Oddly, although the big Ford discarded its almost vestigial 1961 fins in 1962, the all-new intermediate-size Fairlane debuted the same year with fins that looked salvaged from the '61 Ford parts bin. The new intermediates from GM and Chrysler were finless.

The final fins were famously found on the 1964 edition of Cadillac, their putative originator 16 years earlier, and on the Mercury of the same year. The latter came late to the party, first sprouting modest tailfins in 1961.

A Fin in Our Future?

But is the fabled fin forever finished?

Car designers are looking more to the past these days, as evidenced by the Chrysler 300, PT Cruiser, New Beetle, Camaro, Challenger and Mustang revivals, and Chevrolet HHR. On other current cars, more prominent fenders and high beltlines also recall the past.

While styling cues from the mid-20th century are most evident right now, it may be only a matter of time before stylists seeking something new by looking at the old rediscover the 1950s. The retractable hardtop convertibles of the late '50s Ford Skyliners are already making a comeback in Chryslers and Volvos. So we may yet see the revival of chrome trim, two-tone paint, pillarless hardtops, whitewall tires...and tall "stabilizers" sprouting from cars' hind quarters.

With Toyota moving into preeminence in the world automotive market and a death watch remaining for GM, analysts are saying that what Detroit needs to win back customers from Asian rivals is simply more exciting cars. The new car buyer's dreary choice today is between boxy SUVs and boring look-alike jelly bean-shaped sedans. Writing about what he calls "automotive ennui," *Wall Street Journal* auto columnist Joseph B. White concludes that "a lot of the cars sold in the U.S. are just dull. Whose heart leaps at the thought of firing up a Toyota Corolla?"

Exactly 50 years ago a traditional purveyor of dull-as-dishwater vehicles ignited a design revolution with sleek bodies dominated by upswept rear fenders that produced the most exciting looking cars motordom has ever seen. Today that same company — a shadow of its former self and just cast off as a money-loser by one of the world's most prominent car makers — must find a point of differentiation to survive against its giant competitors around the world.

A bold move is needed, and for that Chrysler might do well to look for inspiration to a point in its history when it was suddenly out in front with a model the industry scrambled to follow. The ultimate survival of the MoPar name may or may not involve the rebirth of the tailfin. But it may well necessitate the same kind of sharp break with convention that a half-century ago raised up both the rear quarters of our cars and our level of excitement in seeing and driving them.

John L. Gann, Jr., President of Gann Associates, does consulting in land use regulation. His new manual, How to Prevent Junk Car Laws from Shutting Down Your Home Car Hobby, *offers detailed how-to pointers on making local hobby-friendly regulations happen. Comments or suggestions from readers on future topics to cover relating to local regulation may be sent to Mr. Gann at citykid@uwalumni.com or (800) 762-GANN.*

CHAPTER 4 | 1952-'54 NASH-HEALEY
By Byron Olsen

WELL-TRAVELED NASHES
Crossing the Atlantic to build America's first sports car

Italian designer Pinin Farina (standing) designed a new Nash-Healey for 1952. CEO George Mason is behind the wheel.

This "Motor City Milestone" is perhaps only half qualified for the title, because it was not entirely built in the United States. The Nash-Healey automobile was a unique British-American hybrid built from 1951 through 1954. It is a significant American car, because it was the first genuine sports car conceived and marketed by a mainline American car builder in response to the growing popularity of European sports cars in the United States following World War II.

Led by the MG TC and glamorized by the stunning Jaguar XK-120, British sports cars were stealing the hearts of American car enthusiasts. At first, Detroit tried to dismiss the threat, saying that Americans would never accept the firm ride of most sports cars or give up having room for six passengers. By 1955, Chevrolet introduced the Corvette, Ford was building the two-passenger Thunderbird and Kaiser was making the Darrin KF-161 two-passenger sports car. But the Nash-Healey was first to the market by two years.

The story begins when George Mason,

23

the far-sighted CEO of Nash-Kelvinator, met Donald Healey, the British sports car builder, on a Trans-Atlantic crossing aboard the liner Queen Elizabeth. Mason wanted to jazz up the Nash car line, which he felt had a stodgy reputation. Before the liner docked in New York, Mason and Healey had conceived the Nash-Healey sports car to put some spice in the Nash car line.

The first Nash-Healeys were built in 1951 using a chassis and suspension designed and built by Healey and an English body. Healey had been looking for a big American car engine to power his cars and hoped to buy a modern U.S. overhead-valve V-8. Nash didn't have a V-8 yet, but it did have a robust inline six with overhead valves and seven main bearings used in the topline Nash Ambassador. One of these cars had just placed third in the Mexican Road Race the year before, so using this engine in a sports car did not seem far fetched. In this first Nash-Healey sports car, the engine displaced 235 cubic inches and developed 125 bhp. It was specially equipped with a higher-compression cylinder head and dual SU side-draft carburetors. Nash supplied the engines, three-speed-plus-overdrive transmissions and the rest of the drive train. Nash also built the excellent Weather-Eye heater and other components.

The response to this first model was encouraging enough to inspire Nash to hire famed Italian designer Pinin Farina to design a new Nash-Healey for 1952. Farina was already working for Nash on the 1952 Nash Ambassador and Statesman passenger cars. This new Nash-Healey body design was Nash's own and owed nothing to the previous British body design. The new car was lower with a one-piece curved glass windshield. The headlights were set in the grille, predicting the 1955 Nashes. The bumpers were large and sturdy, a very American feature at the time. There was a leather bench seat with a floor-mounted gear shift. Wheelbase was 102 inches, and overall length 170 inches. The chassis was built by Healey and used Healey's excellent trailing-arm front suspension and a Nash-based coil spring rear. The result was both good handling and a comfortable ride.

The construction process, however, was complex. First, Nash shipped the engine, drivetrain and other components to England where Healey installed them in the chassis. Then, the completed chassis was shipped to Italy where Farina built and installed his newly designed body. The result was slow and limited production, and a high price. The 1951 English-bodied car had a price of $4,063, while the new 1952 Farina-bodied Nash-Healey went up to $5,868. This was in Cadillac territory and scared buyers away.

Midyear, engine displacement was increased to 252 cid and brake horsepower went up to 140 units. Performance benefitted, and the car could now comfortably exceed 100 mph and accelerate briskly. In 1953, a coupe version was added, riding on

This Nash-Healey coupe is believed to be the second version built for 1954, although sources differ. The other version had a rear "C" pillar slanted the other way and a one piece rear window. The car shown here has a three-piece rear window.

a longer 108-inch wheelbase with 10 inches greater length. For 1954, the coupe roof line was redesigned, and prices were dropped somewhat. The last Nash-Healey was built in August 1954.

The principle purpose of the Nash-Healey was to draw attention to Nash cars and build some excitement in Nash showrooms. Nash no doubt knew that the complicated construction process and high prices would never allow volume production or generate high sales. Over the four-year production span, a total of 506 Nash-Healeys were built. They achieved the company's objective at the time, and the cars still look attractive today.

Build quality of the Farina bodies equaled the best of custom coachwork at the time. And the rugged Ambassador engine rang up an amazing competition record on the Healey chassis. Specially bodied Nash-Healeys placed ninth in the 1950 Mille Miglia road race and fourth at Le Mans the same year. At Le Mans in 1951, a Nash-Healey placed third in class and sixth overall, and in 1952, had its best finish yet: third overall. This was an astounding performance for a 20-year-old, everyday-American-sedan-engine design running against the newest and most sophisticated European designs, and some of the newest American overhead-valve V-8 engines.

CHAPTER 5 | **1952 MERCURY**

By Phil Hall

MORE FROM MERCURY

Mercury joined the hardtop craze with new models in 1952

To join the two-door hardtop club for 1952, Mercury offered a pair of models in the popular body style. Above is the base Custom, which was the more popular. There also was a top-line Monterey Special Custom. The small hubcaps indicate the new low-priced status, and the blackwall tires were courtesy of the Korean conflict, which restricted whitewalls when the photo was taken.

Mercury has been a make in search of a mission, and it has been for some time. It was given a short string to find itself in the Ford Motor Co.'s latest survival program. The outcome was extinction.

Introduced as a 1939 model based on the Ford passenger car, Mercury was more or less a gussied-up Ford through 1948. For 1949, the marque received a new body and chassis it shared with Lincoln rather than Ford (except for station wagons).

All that changed for the all-new 1952 models, when again, Mercury was a stepsister to Ford. While the 1949-'51 Mercurys went on to become customizer, cult and collector classics, the style did not adapt itself to the popular two-door hardtop configuration that most of the competitors had in their lineups during Mercury's "bathtub" years.

It should be noted that Hudson had integrated styling similar to Mercury, but it added the Hollywood hardtop to the lineup mid year in 1951. However, Hudson planned to keep its basic form for a few years to come.

For 1952, Mercury would be joined by Lincoln, full-sized Nash, Studebaker and Willys in offering two-door hardtops for the first time; they were the last mass-produced domestic cars to join the party.

While the 1952 Mercury was more contemporary with slab sides, split-level grille and flat hood and front fenders, it was not a stunner.

There was basically one series of models through 1951. However, mid-year 1950 and 1951, the Monterey two-door sedan was added. It was an upscale attempt to compete with the hardtops. For 1952, Mercury was split into two full series: base Custom and top-line Monterey Special Custom. This gave Mercury buyers a choice of lower-priced models for the first time.

Two-door hardtops and four-door sedans populated both series. The Custom received a two-door sedan, and the Monterey added a convertible. There was also a pair of wood-trimmed four-door station wagons in six- and eight-passenger forms.

If the sales literature is to be believed, the Custom hardtop was called the "Sport Coupe" and the Monterey the "Coupe." No matter what they were named, the cheaper version proved the most popular with 30,599 being built. This compared to the Monterey's tally of 24,453. In collector values today, both hardtops are about equal, but well behind the Monterey convertible.

While the outside styling may or may not have been the right thing to do, the instrument panel fit right in with the new jet fighters of the era. The "Interceptor" design featured a panel that protruded from the dash and held the semi-circular speedometer surrounded by gauges and aircraft-like controls on each side for the heating/ventilation system. It continued in revised form through the 1954 models.

Korean conflict restrictions prevented Ford from introducing new overhead-valve V-8s for Ford and Mercury for the all-new 1952 models, so both soldiered on with flatheads. Mercury, at 255.4 cubic inches, produced 125 advertised horses.

Two-door hardtops would stay in the Mercury lineup for decades to come. They would be joined by a Plexiglas-topped version, the Sun Valley, for 1954 and 1955, and Phaeton four-door hardtops mid year in 1956.

As for independence from Ford designs, the 1957-'60 models would be the exception to the lock-step rule that dictated most of Mercury's offerings.

CHAPTER 6 | **1953 BUICK SKYLARK**
By Byron Olsen

BENCHMARK BUICK
GM soared to new heights with the remarkable '53 Skylark

The 1953 Buick Skylark (Model 76X) was based on the Roadmaster convertible (Model 76R), but with several modifications to the body, including sectioned doors, a chopped windshield, cut-open rear wheel openings and special trim, among other features. To accommodate the lower roof and cut-down doors, the seat back was also sectioned and the steering column was lowered.

Few automobiles built in the United States since World War II are more deserving of our love and admiration than the 1953 Buick Skylark, a car that demonstrated the glamour and style that Americans had come to expect from Detroit car builders.

The Skylark was a limited-production, top-of-the-line luxury convertible. It presented several major styling innovations for the first time from an American car maker, innovations that would quickly spread to other models and other makes. It was exciting, it was flashy, it was powerful and it exuded glamour: it was a true star of the 1950s.

Buick division of General Motors was an industry leader by 1950. Led by the dynamic Harlow Curtice (who would become CEO of General Motors), Buick regularly placed fourth in industry sales right behind the "low-priced three" of Chevrolet, Ford and Plymouth. That was quite a feat, because Buicks were priced considerably higher. Buick had, for years, been a major player in the luxury-car field with its Roadmaster and Limited models, cars which competed at the Cadillac and Packard level. The Buick Super, which was firmly established in the upper end of the medium-price field, often led Buick sales. Even the Special, Buick's lowest-priced model, was priced above the Ford/Chevrolet/Plymouth level.

There were several reasons for this sales success. Buicks were seen as having good value. They were big and hefty and looked it; they all had overhead-valve, inline eight-cylinder engines; and they usually carried a lot of chrome. Buicks had a well-cushioned, soft ride, which the public equated with luxury and quality. The ride was the result of coil springs on all four wheels, which sports car enthusiasts claimed made for sloppy handling. But the public loved it.

Buick styling became more and more chrome-laden from 1949 and after. Portholes on the fender sides appeared in 1949. Called "Ventiports" by Buick, the ostensible purpose was to provide additional cooling for the engine compartment. The Ventiports became a standard Buick design feature, but soon became non-functional and merely decorative.

The 1950 grille was a massive affair with nine teeth extending down over the bumper to also serve as bumper guards. This grille soon became the poster child for excessive use of chrome on American cars. Again, the public loved it.

As 1953 approached, GM, as well as Buick, was on a roll. Cadillac and Oldsmobile already had modern, powerful new V-8 engines, and a new V-8 was scheduled for the 1953 Buicks. Spectacular new bodies were planned for 1954 Oldsmobiles, Buicks and Cadillacs. GM design leadership was heavily promoted by the corporation's traveling Motorama car show. At these shows, held around the country, GM showed its latest designs and the latest "dream cars," which we now call concept cars. At the 1953 Motoramas, there was something else: Some dream cars the public could actually buy! One of these dream-come-true cars was the Buick Skylark.

1953 was Buick's golden anniversary year. The Super and Roadmaster entered this significant year with a carryover body design now entering its fourth year of production. Yet Buick did a clever job of restyling its products with a revised grille and new combined headlamps/parking lamps that gave the car a fresh look. The chrome was toned down, and altogether, the cars looked very sharp. The big news was Buick's first V-8. It barely increased the displacement of the previous Roadmaster straight-eight (322 cubic inches versus 320 cubic inches of the old engine), but generated almost 20 more horsepower: 188 bhp. Just as important, the new engine was shorter and weighed 180 lbs. less. The Roadmaster no longer used a chassis and front-end sheet metal that was five inches longer. It now shared these components with the Super. The wheelbase was 121.5 inches and overall length 207.6 inches on all but the four-door.

The Skylark was built using the Roadmaster convertible body and drivetrain. For the Skylark, the doors and rear quarter panels were cut lower at the window sill to give a racy, sports car effect. Inches were also sliced off the top of the windshield, cutting the car height down to less than 59 inches. The rear wheel wells were fully cut out, all the better to display the standard-equipment, genuine chrome wire wheels, which had not been available since the 1930s. The trademark Buick chrome sweep spears, which ran from the front wheel opening to the rear wheel, were greatly slimmed down. And the Ventiports, to critics another symbol of Buick excess, were gone! The exterior appearance of the Skylark was handsome, sporty and glamorous.

Inside, there was a choice of four special leather interiors. Virtually every option was standard, including power steering, power brakes and a signal-seeking radio. Delivered price in the Midwest was a whopping $5,106, compared to $3,479 for the Roadmaster convertible, essentially the same car. The Skylarks were shown at the Motoramas along with two other limited-production luxury convertibles — the Cadillac Eldorado and the Oldsmobile Fiesta. All three were big hits, but the Skylark was far and away the biggest seller with 1,690 cars built. These three cars prepared the buying public for some design features that would appear on many 1954-model GM cars, notably wrap-around, panoramic windshields (seen for the first time on the Fiesta and Eldorado), cut-down doors and, on Buicks, fully cut-out rear wheel openings.

The Skylark was clearly one of the most successful image-building cars that Buick ever built. The Skylark name has been used on thousands of Buicks since, although none have quite measured up to the original. Since it was new, the '53 Skylark has been sought after as a collector car. Today, a 1953 Skylark in No. 1 condition is valued at $184,500 by *Old Cars Price Guide*!

To see current and past values for Buick Skylarks, as well as auction-realized prices for Skylarks going back to 2001, go to www.oldcarsweekly.com/report.

CHAPTER 7 | **1953-'54 KAISER-DARRIN**

By Byron Olsen

A SUCCESSFUL FAILURE
The doomed Kasier-Darrin was really a winner on many fronts

The long hood and swooping curves were trademarks of the of the Kaiser-Darrin.

In the early '50s, thanks to the MG TC and the Jaguar XK-120, sports cars were coming on strong in the United States. American car builders had little experience building true sports cars in the European mold, and the Nash-Healey was the first tentative step by a U.S car company into this market. Another early adventure by an American car builder in the exotic new realm of sports cars was the Kaiser-Darrin 161.

By 1952, the bold attempt by Kaiser-Frazer to become a permanent full-line manufacturer of automobiles in Detroit was running out of steam. After World War II, Henry Kaiser, a successful entrepreneur who had been a major producer of war materials, had joined forces with Joe Frazer, who had long-time experience in the auto business, to start a new car company called Kaiser-Frazer. The company was able to get into volume production of an entirely new line of cars by 1947 to help meet the pent-up demand of the postwar sellers' market, and was an immediate success. By 1952,

31

This shows the sliding doors and very low height of the Kaiser-Darrin. The car was only 36 inches high at the cowl. Tail lamps are from the 1952 Kaiser sedans.

supply had caught up with demand, and Kaiser was having a difficult time meeting the competitive appeal of the "Big Three" car companies with their new V-8 engines. For power, Kaiser had only a 226-cid L-head Continental six-cylinder engine and a limited range of body types to offer. To be sure, Kaiser had introduced an exciting and new low-slung body design for 1951, which most agreed was beautiful. But as the 1953 model year approached, the excitement of the new body could not make up for the lack of excitement in the engine room, and the lack of glamorous new body types such as hardtops, convertibles and station wagons. It looked to industry observers and the public alike that Kaiser would soon go out of business, a view that hurt sales even more.

There was a legendary auto designer, who had played a major role in Kaiser's automotive fortunes, and who now stepped back on stage to design and inspire Kaiser's last great automobile, the Kaiser-Darrin. Howard "Dutch" Darrin had helped design the first Kaisers and Frazers back in 1947 and had played a major role in the design of the beautiful 1951 Kaiser. Darrin's automotive career went back to the 1920s, when he had been a partner in European coachbuilding enterprises of the Classic era. Strong willed and opinionated, Darrin had parted ways with the Kaiser design department and returned to his shop and showroom in Hollywood where, in 1952, he set about designing on his own hook what he thought should be the ultimate Kaiser.

Darrin started with the chassis from the Henry J car, a compact Kaiser model that had sold poorly. Darrin had had little to do with the design of the Henry J, and didn't like it, but said the Henry J chassis "deserved something better than it had received." Wheelbase was a short 100 inches.

Darrin conceived a stunning two-seat sports car body for it, with a long, curving hood, a dipped window sill line and a three-position convertible top. The dipped sill line was a Darrin trademark, often referred to as "the Darrin dip." The top could be partly folded to just open the area over the seats. But the most significant features of the car were the doors and the body construction: it was one of the first uses of fiberglass, and the doors opened by sliding forward into the fenders, rather than opening outward! The lovely teardrop taillights from the 1952 Kaiser full-size cars completed the attractive picture.

Darrin used Henry J mechanicals including a modest 161-cid L-head six-cylinder engine which was actually designed and built by Willys. It sounds anemic to us today, but remember, there were no small-block V-8s around then. The engine was mildly hopped up and firmer springs and shocks were specified. The resulting package managed to have good handling and decent performance, because it was so light weight. The fiberglass body weighed only about 300 lbs. and the total car weighed only 2,175 lbs.

Darrin had planned to try to interest Kaiser in his new sports car, but was prepared to produce it himself, if the company was not interested. He showed his baby to the Kaisers, Henry and son Edgar, in the fall of 1952. Before long, Kaiser had decided to put the Darrin sports car into production, even though the rest of the Kaiser product line was faltering badly, and would cease U.S. production entirely by 1955. Meanwhile, the new sports car, christened the Kaiser-Darrin, was shown at auto shows and to the motoring press during 1953 and put into production by the end of the year. Reviews were generally favorable, and fiberglass was seen as the coming thing, because GM was showing prototypes of the forthcoming Corvette at the same time.

It is interesting to compare the first three sports cars put into production by American manufacturers after World War II. The Nash-Healey (reviewed in the previous "Motor City Milestone" column), the Chevrolet Corvette and the Kaiser-Darrin. All three were powered by in-line six cylinder engines, two of the three were made of fiberglass, and all three of the convertible models had wheelbases around 100 inches. The Darrin was the longest, but far and away the lightest weight. The Nash-Healey and the Corvette had engines 70 to 90 cid larger and so handily outperformed the Darrin, in spite of its lighter weight.

The Kaiser-Darrin had another problem. Like the Nash-Healey, because of the hand-built nature of its production, the price was high enough to scare away many prospective buyers. But mainly Kaiser cars were on death row by this time and buyers were steering clear of anything with the Kaiser name. During 1954, 435 Kaiser-Darrins were built, plus an indeterminate number of prototypes and "experimentals." As Kaiser automobile production wound down late in 1954, Darrin found about 100 completed Kaiser-Darrins laying around the factory at Willow Run, Mich. He bought 50 of them and sold them through his Los Angeles showroom over the next several years. He equipped some with 304-bhp Cadillac engines and some were raced on the SCCA sports car circuit. After that, the Kaiser-Darrins were all gone, and it was all over. It was too bad an exciting design like the Kaiser-Darrin sports car did not have a better chance to find a market.

CHAPTER 8 | 1953-'54 PLYMOUTH
By John Lee

TOO LITTLE, TOO EARLY?
For 1953-'54, Plymouth tried a smaller approach

Jerry Fletcher added some mild custom touches while restoring his 1953 Plymouth convertible. Besides a factory-optional continental kit, flush-fit skirts and wire wheel covers, he dechromed the hood, deleted the front bumper guards and swapped to 1954 headlight rims.

If you had been shopping for a new convertible in 1953 or 1954, would your local Plymouth dealer have been on the list of places to visit?

If you were looking for a restoration project from the 1950s, or a restored car to drive and enjoy, would you walk past a Bel Air or a Sunliner ragtop to check out a Cambridge or a Belvedere?

Not too likely on either count. In the first place, Ford sold some 75,000 convertibles in 1953-'54 and Chevy sold almost 45,000, while Plymouth moved just more than 13,000. Which will probably also answer the second question, because with that degree of rarity, chances of finding one either restored or unrestored slim down quickly.

Yet, seeing one nicely finished, especially with a pair of mellow glasspack mufflers (no, they were not even a factory option, but who cares?) and optional wire wheels, is enough to make one ask, "Why not?"

Certainly, there was some grumbling among the Plymouth faithful in 1953 about their favorite marque having shrunk. Anyone looking to trade up from their 1949-'52

34

All 1953 and 1954 Plymouth two-doors featured 2/3-1/3 split front seats for easier back seat access.

"full-size" Plymouth would be taking a cut from 118 1/2 inches to 114 inches in wheelbase length and nearly five inches in overall body length.

The new platform was a compromise. For the economy-minded, Plymouth had been marketing a smaller, less-expensive model for the past four years. The Deluxe (1949-'50) and Concord (1951-'52) models — Nash offered only as a single-seat business coupe, fastback two-door sedan and two-door Suburban station wagon — rode a 111-inch wheelbase. So, the single wheelbase length of 114 inches for 1953 fell between the two previous spans. It was an inch shorter than that of rivals Ford and Chevrolet.

The two-year 1953-'54 Plymouth model run is in a class of its own.

Separate, detachable rear fenders that were so 1940s were finally eliminated. New slab-side styling gained character from subtle, horizontal flares over the front and rear wheel openings, which were decorated with bright stainless trim on the upscale models. The front flares continued around the front fenders, right into the horizontal grille bar, while those in back wrapped around the quarter panels and across the rear panel just below the trunk opening. The license plate mounted in the center of the panel and the gas filler opening was on the left.

For the first time, Plymouths had curved, one-piece windshields, and one-piece wrap-

The facelift for 1954 included connecting front and rear fender trim spears with additional stainless strips, and new rear fender gravel guards.

around rear glass on two-door hardtops.

The face 1953 Plymouths presented in dealer showrooms featured a single horizontal grille bar with the ends painted to match the body, a bright stainless center section and nine vertical trim pieces wrapping around it. Stainless headlamp rims fit flush with the fenders, and rectangular parking lamps below followed the contour of the grille bar.

The facelift stylists provided to change the frontal look for 1954 with a new chrome center grille bar section featuring the Plymouth name in plastic, and horizontal bright trim that wrapped around and connected with the front fender trim. A thinner stainless trim bar below the main bar spanned the grille opening between round parking lamps. The chrome '54 headlamp rims tunnelled the lenses about an inch.

Slightly restyled tail lamps incorporated round back-up lamps, and chrome bolt-on fins added visual length to the rear fenders. Stats on these two models showed the '54s, at 193 1/2 inches, measure four inches longer than the '53s. Although the bodies are the same, the rear bumpers have been moved out from the body, a slight alteration to make the cars look (and measure) a bit longer. It seems the '53s looked too stubby for some customers.

Adding stainless-steel trim strips connecting the front and rear fender trim may have made the '54 Savoys and Belvederes look longer, but I always thought it was unnecessary and looked cheap. A better $37.65 add-on for convertibles and hardtops came in the spring of 1954, along with new, bright spring colors. A narrow trim strip dropped down from the beltline at the front of the doors, trailed back at a slightly downward angle and kicked back up to the beltline at the rear of the window opening. With a basket-weave insert, this trim offered a two-tone accent and hinted of a sports car-style beltline dip.

The interiors were improved for 1954 with nicer and more colorful upholstery fabrics, brighter dashboard trim and a new deluxe steering wheel.

The well-known 217.8-cid flathead six was rated at an even 100 hp for both years. Options for the standard three-speed transmission were overdrive or the semi-automatic HyDrive. In April, 1954, Plymouth finally received a fully automatic transmission with the offering of the two-speed PowerFlite at $189. Along with PowerFlite, Plymouth installed the Dodge Division's 230-cid, 110-hp six.

Plymouth series names were juggled between 1953 and 1954. Belvedere, identification for the two-door hardtop model since 1951, now named the entire top trim series consisting of the convertible, a hardtop, a four-door sedan and a Suburban wagon. Savoy, which had named a high-trim Suburban in 1952 and 1953, now designated the entire middle-trim-level series, and the economy-level series adopted a new name: Plaza.

Even before World War II ended, Plymouth engineering and marketing personnel had seemed insistent that there should be a market for a smaller, lighter, more economical automobile. They had toyed with small-car designs, then built the shorter-wheelbase 1949-'52 Deluxe and Concord models before unleashing the seemingly sensible-sized 1953-'54s.

It may have been a case of designing a car for a market that didn't exist, or maybe the first example of "build it and they will come." The 1953 production total of 636,000 was a new all-time high for the Plymouth Division, but that figure headed the wrong way, dropping to 433,000 for the facelifted 1954 models. The 13,200 convertibles built in those two years was a slight drop from the 15,650 sold in 1951-'52.

CHAPTER 9 | **1954 DODGE ROYAL 500**

By John Lee

PICKING UP THE PACE
1954 Dodge Royal 500 pace car offers stiff restoration challenge

Dodge built a total of 701 replicas of the 1954 Royal 500 Indianapolis 500 Pace Car. This one was completely restored and sold in the Barrett-Jackson Scottsdale auction last January.

What collector doesn't dream of owning a flashy, top-of-the-line model of their favorite make? What it takes to get it back to its original showroom shine might not even cross their mind.

Restoring a special model, such as a 1954 Dodge Royal 500 convertible pace car, can often present special challenges. On the plus side, laying out a pile of dough for such an expensive, low-production prize might have encouraged the first buyer to keep it in prime condition. Such was not the case with this Dodge ragtop, however, which Bob Felthousen bought, restored to 99.9-point perfection, then sold in order to pursue other projects.

Felthousen traced this pace car back to Torgelsen Brothers Dodge in Anaconda, Mont., where it was posed on an elevated ramp in the showroom. The 89-year-old former salesman that Felthousen talked to said he sold it to a rancher who gave it to his son as a graduation present. A young man with a fast, flashy car in which he has invested none of his own sweat or savings is not the formula for a pampered life. The car's first years were spent driving on — and off — country roads, as well as over hills and, as scars attested, even went through a barbed-wire fence at some time.

When the transmission went out in 1959, it went into a mechanic's garage. Twenty years later, after both the rancher owner and the mechanic had died, the Dodge reportedly was sold at auction for $15. It languished with the next owner for several more years before Felthousen acquired it through a friend. No stranger to tough undertakings, the retired heavy equipment contractor went right to work on the Dodge. Fortunately, many special items, such as the wire wheels and continental spare tire kit, were still with the car, but lots of small parts had to be found or, in some cases, made.

Dodging competition with a Hemi

Dodge began carving a new image with the 1953 introduction of its 241-cid overhead-valve V-8. With the Hemi-head Red Ram engine, Dodge topped all American eight-cylinder cars in the 1953 Mobilgas Economy Run, and a few months later, a '54 model set 196 AAA stock car speed records at the Bonneville Salt Flats. Six NASCAR wins in 1953 were the first for Dodge.

Dodge convertibles, hardtops and two-door wagons were all built on a 114-inch wheelbase, the same as Plymouth, during the 1953-'54 model run. Meanwhile, sedans and four-door wagons had a 118-inch wheelbase.

The emerging performance image prompted Indianapolis 500 officials to grant Dodge the privilege of pacing the 1954 race. A specially equipped yellow convertible led the field of 33 racers to their rolling start at The Brickyard. Dean Martin and Jerry Lewis, the most popular comedy team at the time, have been pictured riding in the car at the Indy track.

Dodge gave the pace car a new Royal 500 model designation, with chrome "500" lettering placed above the rear fender gravel shields and crossed flags on the front fenders and deck lid. Appearance was further dolled up with a continental spare wheel carrier, black color sweep dropping down from the window line and 15-inch chrome wire wheels. Fitting the 241-cid Hemi with a four-barrel carburetor and dual exhausts boosted its output to 170 hp, 20 more than the standard two-barrel engine.

Restoring the rare pace car

Dodge built 701 replicas of the 1954 pace car for sale to the public. Felthousen knows of only about a dozen survivors. Unaware of the convertible's different-size body, he bought a '54 Dodge four-door parts car and "nothing interchanged." He ended up heating and shrinking dents in the front fenders and metal finishing all body panels without using plastic filler. Fortunately, in spite of rough use, the convertible had spent its entire life on the dry high plains and had no rust. Yet, there were some surprises.

"We found about 20 lbs. of dog food in the frame rails that mice had carried in," he noted.

The hardest parts to find were the taillamp reflectors. Felthousen finally obtained a pair from Canada. He lucked out by locating a new fiberglass heater air intake box and several pieces missing from the continental spare from an enthusiast who had bought out a dealer's parts stock in western Nebraska.

The most expensive items were the molded black vinyl trim pieces on the top inside of the doors.

"I had to have a company make a mold and reproduce them," Felthousen said. "Fortunately, another guy restoring a pace car needed some, too, so we split the cost."

Replicating the Indy 500 lettering was another chore that most restorers don't encounter. Felthousen took old photos of the original pace car to a sign shop in his home town of Plattsmouth, Neb., where they were scanned onto a computer. Then, using known measurements, such as the length of a door handle, the lettering was reproduced as decals that the maker claims are within .003-inch of the originals.

After the 18-month restoration was completed, Felthousen showed the pace car several times, receiving an AACA First Junior Award.

After spending a few years with another owner, the Dodge was sold at the Barrett-Jackson auction in Scottsdale in January of this year. Felthousen said he'd be glad to hear from the new owner, because he still has the car's complete history, including a photo of it in the original dealer's showroom.

To read more about Royal 500s and other Dodge collector cars, check out the CD "Standard Catalog of Chrysler: 1914-2000," at www.oldcarsbookstore.com

CHAPTER 10 — 1954 FORD CRESTLINE
By Phil Hall

1954 CRESTLINE FORDOR

A new addition to Ford's Crestline series for 1954 was the Fordor sedan. It gave the make a luxury entry in the low-priced field that year. It was the most popular of the Crestline models then, but it's the least-valued and sought today. (Phil Hall collection)

Of the several notable changes to the 1954 Ford passenger cars, one of the less-remembered is the addition of a four-door sedan to the Crestline series. For 1952 and 1953, the top-end Crestline lineup was home to the Sunliner convertible, Victoria two-door hardtop and wood-and-vinyl-trimmed Country Squire four-door station wagon. Moving forward to 1954, those models continued to use the same bodies and chassis.

Adding the common body style, which Ford called the Fordor, was a subtle recognition that a market existed for a taste of luxury in the low-priced field for the family that didn't go for the sportier hardtops, convertibles and wagons. It was also a not-so-subtle recognition that Chevrolet did much the same thing in 1953 with its Bel Air four-door sedan. The Bel Air series also had a two-door sedan in its top series, something Ford would address in 1955.

In 1952 and 1953, the fanciest four-door sedan in the Ford line was the mid-level Customline. In the year before that, having a four-door sedan in the top series was com-

41

mon for Ford, but the demotion for 1952 indicated the company chose to elevate only its specialty models.

Among the features of the Crestline sedan were additional exterior trim, two-tone interiors featuring Arrowhead upholstery, a rear robe cord, colored steering wheel and column and full carpeting. Options like rear fender skirts, full wheel covers, power seat, power windows and power steering and brakes all made the Crestline Fordor an attractive package, especially when it cost just over $100 more than the Customline counterpart.

When the production numbers were figured out, the Fordor was the most popular Crestline model with 99,677 sold. This compared to 95,464 for the Victoria, 33,685 for the Sunliner and 12,797 for the Country Squire.

There was a fifth Crestline model for 1954, the also-new Skyliner, which, among today's collectors, ranks right up there with the Sunliner as the most valuable of the year's offerings. It had a green-tint Plexiglas fixed-roof panel over the front seat with a detachable inner liner. The feature would return to the Ford lineup in 1955 and 1956, but the concept, in fixed and sliding forms, would return on other makes and is popular to this day.

Ford's 1954 car line was the recipient of its first overhead-valve V-8, called the Y-Block. It replaced (except in Canada) the flathead V-8 that served since 1932. It was sized at 239 cubic inches, the same as the flathead, but would eventually grow to 312 cubic inches. The simple 1954 rating with a two-barrel carburetor was 130 horsepower.

Along with Ford's modern (first seen in the 1952 models) overhead-valve six, the V-8 gave the company an advantage over Chevrolet and Plymouth for a year, as both had only sixes of dated design. For 1954, Ford offered both the six and V-8 in all Crestline models, a first for the series, as only the V-8 was available the previous two seasons.

Another plus in the low-priced field was a new ball joint front suspension. It was based on the version Lincoln installed in its new 1952 models.

The dashboard of the 1954 Ford was also notable with its Astra-Dial Control Panel, which featured a plastic panel on the back of the speedometer that emitted daylight, not unlike the Skyliner roof. At night it was lit conventionally. A panel in the Crestliner dash was also trimmed in bright metal.

While the 1954 Ford was attractive in the low-priced field, it was merely doing set-up work for the much face-lifted 1955 models, which featured wraparound windshields, two-tone side trim in the Fairlane (which replaced the Crestline) and more-powerful V-8s.

Today, the 1954 Fords look rather mundane in relation to what came after them. Also today, the Crestline Fordor is nearly forgotten. It holds the least collector value and interest among the Crestline series and is even a step or two behind a couple of lower-priced models of that year.

CHAPTER 11 / **1954 MERCURY XM-800**
By Todd Haefer

EXCELLENT EXPERIMENT
Restored Mercury *XM-800* one of few concept survivors

The 1954 Mercury Monterey *XM-800* was Mercury's first full-fledge concept car. Like other '50s Ford Motor Co. concepts, many of the *XM-800*'s design features made it to production cars, such as the hooded headlamps, skirted wheel openings and rear bumper and taillamp design, which appeared on 1956 Lincolns. The *XM-800*'s roof band appeared on 1955-'56 Ford Crown Victorias.

Few early concept cars have survived to the present. Some were just plain neglected. Others were actually destroyed by manufacturers who didn't want to share any engineering secrets.

Mercury's 1954 Monterey *XM-800* concept is an exception, thanks to the efforts of Tom Maruska of Duluth, Minn., who completed his restoration of the one-of-a-kind car in 2009 and debuted it at the Meadow Brook Concourse d'Elegance in Rochester Hills, Mich.

"It was by far the most challenging project I have ever worked on," said Maruska, who is known for several other restorations, including the 1963 Thunderbird Italian concept that sold for $600,000 and a 1964 Amphicar that sold for $124,000.

Before Maruska found it, the *XM-800* ("XM" for "Experimental Mercury") sat in muck up to its floorboards outside a Michigan farmhouse for decades, hosting genera-

The XM-800 after its recent restoration.

tions of mice and other critters — Maruska even had to remove acorns from the engine block. The wiring had been torn out and the roof had caved in from snowfalls. A hole had been drilled in the center of the roof depression, allowing melting snow and rainfall to run into the car's interior.

It was a sad existence for the concept that wowed the auto show circuit in 1954, making headlines wherever it went and even appearing in the movie "Woman's World" with Fred MacMurray, June Allyson and Lauren Bacall.

The *XM-800*, originally intended to be called the Javelin, was designed in the Mercury Pre-Production Studio in 1952 by John Najjar, the manager of the studio, and Elwood Engle, a design consultant. It was built in October 1953 and introduced during the February 1954 Detroit Auto Show.

It featured the first use of fins on a Ford, the first Ford tachometer and the first time for front and rear bucket seats. While it never made it to production, some of its stylings, such as forward-slanted, hooded headlamps; covered front wheels; and its slender, canted taillamp-rear and bumper-exhaust combo, were modified for use on the 1956 Lincoln. Other styling cues appeared on 1955 and 1957 Lincolns.

After the *XM-800* finished its circuit, Ford donated it in 1956 to the University of Michigan, where it was used as a teaching tool in auto design classes.

It was originally thought that UM students installed a new deep-dish steering wheel with a shorter steering column, which was thought to be more energy absorbing in an accident than the original flat-type steering wheel.

Maruska, however, found out that this was done by Ford in 1955, before the school donation — showing the company was still using the *XM-800* for experiments in safety modifications after its debut.

The university auctioned off the car in 1960 to an unknown person, who brought it to the Michigan farmer for storage. The man paid a year's rent and was never heard from again. The farmer eventually moved the car outside.

In 1979, 17-year-old Dan Brooks and a friend saw the *XM-800* sitting outside the farmer's barn and found out after some research how rare the car was. They asked the farmer if they could buy it and received a big surprise when he gave it to them just to get it off of his property.

Brooks eventually paid his friend $100 to own the car outright and planned on restoring it, but found out that just the chrome plating would cost more than $10,000. He decided to sell it and advertised it for $30,000. He continuously turned down lower offers, but after several years, sold it to concept car collector Joe Bortz of Chicago in 1987.

Bortz also planned on restoring the car, but after getting it running and putting a working transmission in it, sold it to Maruska in 2008.

The car gave Maruska many surprises — some good, some bad. After decades of sitting outside the farmhouse, there was little rust to contend with, since the *XM-800's* body and most of its exterior trim were made from fiberglass. Even the bumpers were chrome-plated fiberglass.

Maruska said the *XM-800* was Ford's first venture into fiberglass and the company may have been the first to try chrome plating it.

"I thought the fiberglass was kind of neat when I was under the car for the first time with the seats removed," he said. "I could see light through the floors and it wasn't due to rust holes!"

He said the most trouble he had with restoration was the electrical system.

"The original wiring was cut apart in at least six places — I suspect Ford might have done that on purpose to protect trade secrets," he said. "That, coupled with the wiring on which the casing had rotted away and-or was eaten by mice, and the fact that the wiring was complex to begin with, made that part of the restoration a real nightmare."

The car featured an electrical trunk and hood unlocking and opening system that was automatically controlled by switches on the dash, and automatically through a 115-volt timer in the trunk, plus power window and seat controls.

After disassembling the *XM-800* last year, Maruska starting refinishing the chassis and suspension in November 2008. His first order of business was scrubbing the whole interior with bleach and dish detergent and rinsing it with a 3,000-psi pressure washer. He rebuilt the transmission himself, but stripped the engine of add-on parts and sent the main engine and heads to a machine shop for rebuilding.

The car retains its original V-8 312 Y-block engine.

"It was rebuilt, but there wasn't too much that had to be done with it," Maruska said. "It still has the original camshaft and no one even had to bore it out."

The transmission, however, is not original, since the *XM-800* was never a running vehicle — there was only an empty case when it was introduced, a common cost-saving measure for concept cars. Maruska just happened to have one from a 1956 Thunderbird that bolted right in.

"The firewall was only an inch away from the back of the engine and there was no room for standard shifting," he said. "I put in a throttle cable used in street rods."

Maruska also found that the White Pearl color thought to be the car's original color was not.

"While removing the paint from the body with aircraft stripper for fiberglass, I discovered that the *XM-800* had been painted a gold metallic color before the White Pearl," he said. "I suspect Ford tried that color first and didn't care for it. An excellent decision, in my opinion. I stayed with the White Pearl."

Maruska has a very detailed online restoration diary with images on his Web site at www.tbirdsquare.com; it also includes a rare 1954 video of the *XM-800* and You Tube links to video restoration footage.

Maruska said that, although he intends to sell the *XM-800*, he's content right now to display it at shows and enjoy the fruits of his labor.

"The *XM-800* really is a piece of artwork and fits perfectly with the art deco movement of its time," he said. "I really don't know what it's worth, but comparable 1950s-era GM concept cars have sold north of $3 million in recent years."

Author Todd Haefer is the editor of Quicksilver, a club magazine published by the International Mercury Owners' Association (www.mercuryclub.com). This car sold at auction in January 2010 for $429,000.

CHAPTER 12 | **1954 CHEVROLET NOMAD**

By Ron Kowalke, photos by Zane Zander

RE-CREATING CHEVY'S MOTORAMA NOMAD

Owner Zane Zander's attention to detail had his Nomad (above) positioned for its 2007 brochure photographs in the same manner as the original was at the 1954 Motorama (left). Externally, there is almost no way to differentiate this recreation from the original Nomad.

It lingers as one of the great unsolved postwar automotive mysteries. What really happened to the 1954 Chevrolet *Nomad* concept car that stunned audiences at each of the five stops of General Motors' 1954 Motorama show? Also known as the Waldorf *Nomad* due to its initial appearance at New York City's famed Waldorf-Astoria Hotel, the Corvette-styled two-door hardtop station wagon prototype is thought to have been destroyed by GM decree sometime in the late 1950s.

But just as rumor remains strong that Elvis has not left the building, old car enthusiasts want to believe that the original Chevy *Nomad* concept also still exists. As with other GM concept cars on which a post-Motorama death sentence was imposed and have since emerged from hiding, similar hope remains for the Waldorf *Nomad*. Hope that it's possibly hidden under a dusty tarp in some long-forgotten Michigan

The original Waldorf *Nomad* (right) as it was displayed at one of the five big-city stops on the circuit of General Motors' 1954 Motorama. The stops were New York City, Miami, Los Angeles, San Francisco and Chicago. Above is the same view of the re-created car.

warehouse, placed there by some forward-thinking GM employee who couldn't stand to see a genuine piece of history destroyed.

While the old car hobby waits for the original *Nomad* — and Elvis — to be found, Brillion, Wis., Chevrolet enthusiast Zane Zander did the next best thing – he built his own Waldorf Nomad. And just as the original did over 50 years ago, Zander's version recently stunned the audience at its initial event appearance at the Minneapolis/St. Paul Auto Show held March 10-18 at the Minneapolis Convention Center.

After getting exposure on the local Minneapolis television news stations, Zander said, "People came to the show just to see the Nomad. It was really popular."

While Zander can now take his completed Nomad on the collector car show circuit and relax and explain to spectators the history of the car, both the original and his version, it's a well-earned time in the spotlight, too. It took Zander and a host of family and friend volunteers almost eight years to complete the project. And it was a nail-biter right to the end.

With the car needing to be at the Minneapolis/St. Paul Auto Show by set-up day on March 8, 2007, the Nomad was still having the finishing touches applied to its upholstery two days prior. It then had to be photographed for a four-color brochure Zander

Much fabrication work was needed to transform the car's original 1955 Pontiac Safari body shell into a *Nomad* look-alike. Here, patch panels are welded in to replicate the curvature of the rear wheel opening.

created that showcases both the original and his Nomad to give out at the auto show. The ink on the brochures was still drying as they and the Nomad were loaded for their trip to Minnesota.

Hands-on engineering

Zander's car-collecting passion is focused on Chevrolets. While he previously owned a '54 Corvette in 1959, his collection never included a much-wanted Nomad. Instead of searching for a popular tri-Chevy version to buy, he decided in the mid-1990s to research the possibility of recreating the original Motorama Corvette *Nomad*.

"I just thought it was really neat," Zander said of the original. "[Recreating the concept] seemed like an achievable goal." Through the entire span of time it took to complete the project, Zander said the committment was "to duplicate the [original] as close as possible." And now that it's done, Zander stressed, "Car for car, it's awfully close."

With no original car from which to pattern, and the fact that the concept *Nomad* was a non-operational display car, Zander was forced to make a few concessions to complete his version of the Nomad and stay within his predetermined budget.

Calling the construction of the car "a good ol' boy project," Zander explained that the design of the car was "mostly in my head; there was no computer involved." He added, "It's what I call 'hands-on engineering'."

Countless hours went into shaping the recreation's body panels to arrive at this stage of primer. This view is probably not that different looking from the original when the GM concept design team created it in their facility in 1953.

Chevrolet enthusiast Zane Zander poses with his *Nomad*, which he and a host of volunteers built for both show and go.

Pontiac to Chevy transformation

Starting with a 1955 Pontiac Safari two-door station wagon frame and body shell, its lengthy transformation to the finished Nomad began in late 1999. While Zander's quest to keep his Nomad as close to the original was paramount, there was one major point of deviation that was agreed upon from day one. Zander said his recreation is "made to go down the road."

To this end, the Safari's frame was boxed, and its front clip was removed and replaced with one donated by a 1977 Chevy Camaro. This serves a two-fold purpose. First, it allowed a Chevy 350-cid V-8 to be fitted for power. Second, for safety reasons, the newer Camaro setup features disc brakes for more reliable stopping.

To the outsider, it might seem that creating a two-door station wagon body from a donor two-door station wagon would be a simple procedure, but this is where the bulk of the recreation's fabrication work took place. The Pontiac shell had to have 3-1/2 inches sectioned from it horizontally to achieve a lower overall stance. The aftermarket fiberglass front bodywork had to be widened two inches, adding one inch to each side to maintain proper fit. The Pontiac's rocker panels, door handles, fuel filler door and rear fender wheel openings all had to be extensively reshaped or totally recreated to mimic those of the original *Nomad*. One of the major challenges was merging the Safari's two-piece tailgate into a one-piece unit that allowed the window glass to lower into the gate, which was one of the bally-hooed elements of the Motorama *Nomad*.

Another challenge posed itself when it came time for Zander to select the recreation's interior fabric. "No one could give me any direction on this," he explained. Photos of the original car showed only partial views of the *Nomad*'s interior. To make matters worse, these photos were all black and white. What Zander eventually selected was a silver-blue colored vinyl that was stitched into the car using the period-correct "French seaming" method. Zander also proudly stated that this was the only part of the build process that was done outside of his Brillion shop.

Zander also selected his *Nomad*'s exterior paint colors to match those of the original car, which featured a silver-blue base with an off-white roof. According to Zander, the base color he chose is called Frost and adorned many 1959 Corvettes. The top's off-white color is the original shade used on '54 Corvettes.

Down the road

With his Nomad finished and having garnered positive reviews in Minnesota, Zander took time to reflect on this long-term project. He said, "I've gained a newfound respect for the guys who build hot rods and customs. It's a tremendous investment of time and ingenuity. Everything we touched [needed] a modification of some kind – what I refer to as 'constant opportunity'." He jokingly added, "I'm going to go back to restoring [cars], where you just replace parts."

For those car enthusiasts who want to learn more about the building of Zander's *Nomad* recreation, he's in the process of creating a Web site at www.waldorfnomad.com that will come online soon.

CHAPTER 13 | **1955 CHICAGO AUTO SHOW**

Story by Mitch Frumkin and Phil Hall
Photos by Chicago Automobile Trade Association

GLITTER & GLAMOUR
Back in '55, Chicago showcased an automotive revolution

Twice daily, a free stage extravaganza was held on the Chicago International Amphitheatre's main floor 29,000-sq. ft. center arena. There was seating for 10,000-12,000 people and more for those standing in the arena. At left, the 1955 Nash was on stage in the Motorevue, along with one of the 20 Community Queens.

Walking from a parking into the Chicago Amphitheatre must have felt like a black-and-white Dorothy opening the door upon landing in the colorful land of Oz. The dreary world of snowy 1954-and-older cars outside the Amphitheatre hardly compared to the new world inside the building, where vast expanses of glass, bright multi-color combinations and V-8 engines ruled the cars displayed by every American automaker during the 1955 Chicago Auto Show.

The 47th Chicago Auto show, which ran from Jan. 8-16, 1955, was one of pure excitement, as the new models on display featured, for the most part, revolutionary change in style, powerplants and engineering, all at one time.

Eighteen domestic brands of cars and eight brands of new trucks were displayed in the Chicago Amphitheatre at 42nd and Halsted streets on the Windy City's south side.

All Chrysler Corp. cars, Chevrolets (except Corvette) and Pontiacs were all-new that year. Having major revisions were Ford, Mercury and Packard offerings. Showing for the first time was the Nash-based Hudson from American Motors. Dream cars were everywhere, as were mid-year models. Modern overhead-valve V-8s were under the hoods of Chevrolet, Pontiac, Plymouth, Nash, Hudson and Packard vehicles for the first time. Color was king inside and out, with two- and three-tone combinations being splashed with vigor and imagination.

Since it started in 1901, the Chicago Auto Show was the nation's showcase for the newest of the new. Starting in 1935, the Chicago Automobile Trade Association-sponsored show was moved to the 225,000-square-foot Chicago International Amphitheatre, an ideal location, even if it was next to the aromatic Chicago Stockyards.

"It was like an enormous jewel case with the vehicles the jewels," said Jerry H. Cizek, the show committee chairman and grandfather of the current show chairman, Jerry H. Cizek III.

Cars and related displays were on the second level, and a wide variety of trucks

Don Koehler, generally recognized at the time as the tallest man in the world at 8 feet, 2-1/2 inches, towers over a Chevrolet Two-Ten coupe.

resided on the ground floor, along with engineering exhibits and special vehicles. Show goers that year were no doubt challenged on where to begin their journey.

General Motors

One could easily have started a tour of passenger cars at the show with the biggest manufacturer, General Motors. Unlike today, where corporate displays are usually side by side, GM and others spread out their brand showcases.

At the time, GM Motorama dream cars were a popular attraction, and displayed at the 1955 show were the *Chevrolet Nomad*, *Pontiac Bonneville Special*, *Oldsmobile F-88*, *Buick Wildcat II* and *Cadillac El Camino*.

The Packard exhibit featured a Four-Hundred two-door hardtop, shown in the center, while the front clip of a Clipper four-door is seen on the lower left foreground. Directly to the right of the Four-Hundred is a side view of the Request show car, and at the rear is the Patrician that was run 25,000 trouble-free miles.

All-new for 1955 were the Chevrolet and Pontiac passenger cars, complete with the almost-mandatory Panoramic windshield. Each series received new V-8s, and Pontiac lost its long-lived six. Oldsmobile, Buick and Cadillac were in their second year of the styling cycle. However, Oldsmobile and Buick showed their new, mid-year four-door hardtops for the first time, the Buick Riviera and Oldsmobile Holiday. Oldsmobile, Buick and Cadillac were among the majority with higher horsepower for 1955. It was at the start of the "horsepower race," after all.

GM also showed off some of its overseas products at the 1955 show, including German Opel, British Vauxhall and Australian Holden. For Opel and Vauxhall, it proved to be a preview, as they weren't officially imported here until 1957.

Chrysler Corp.

Chrysler Corp. products took a beating in the 1954 model year with dated styling and trim combinations. That changed big time when Virgil Exner's all-new 1955 models came out. They were the proverbial longer, lower and wider, all with wraparound windshields, envelope sides and modern drivelines.

Plymouth's "For the Young at Heart" of-

One of the Chicago Auto Show's 20 community beauty queens, 18-year-old Mary Lou Koeppe (Miss Portage Park), posed next to the new Dodge Custom Royal Lancer V-8 during the Motorevue musical stage presentation.

ferings were the most changed, with new V-8 power and styling at least the equal of its competitors. Dodge shared Plymouth's body shell and enhanced its Red Ram V-8 arsenal. A mid-year LaFemme hardtop package was shown, a bold move at the time to appeal to the female buyer. De Soto, Chrysler and the new stand-alone Imperial made use of the same shell, but each had distinctive features. Chrysler Corp. billed its offerings as having the "100 Million Dollar Look." All Chrysler Corp. cars were available with a dash-mounted control lever for their Powerflite automatic transmissions.

Color and expressive side trim two-toning (except on Imperial) was a work in progress during the 1955 model year, and mid-year changes were apparent on Dodge, De Soto and Chrysler, all of which spread top-line chrome and color sweeps to lower-priced models.

Ford Motor Co.

Ford and Mercury largely used 1952-'54 body shells for sedans, but disguised them well and spiced up their lineups with low-profile coupes: The Ford Crown Victoria and Skyliner and Mercury Montclair hard-

All Chrysler-brand cars for 1955 were entirely new from bumper to bumper. In the center of the Chrysler exhibit sat the Imperial two-door hardtop. Imperial was a stand-alone make starting in 1955.

Along with all of its 1955 "finest cars for today" production models, Lincoln displayed one of the Mexican Road Race 1954 Lincoln stock car champions. On hand was driver Walt Faulkner, who took part in the victory.

Below, appearing for the last time at the Chicago Auto Show in 1955 were the cars from Kaiser-Willys. Willys facelifted its Custom four-door sedan and Bermuda hardtop, while the Kaiser Manhattan in the background was the same as the 1954 version. Above, the 1955 Ford and Studebaker trucks share a display area.

top and Sun Valley. Mercury announced its new mid-year Montclair four-door sedan at the show, which used the low roof of the two-doors. Ford's Thunderbird made its second appearance at the show, having been displayed in 1954 as well.

Lincoln cars were a bit longer for 1955, but the models retained their non-wrap windshield from previous years, since an all-new model was coming for 1956. However, Lincoln's display was not lacking for interest, as the *Futura* dream car (think future Batmobile) pulled in crowds. A Mexican Road Race-winning 1954 Lincoln, along with driver Walt Faulkner, was one of the few factory racing displays. However, a new transmission for 1955 meant Lincolns could not race competitively. It didn't matter; the 1955 race was canceled.

Studebaker-Packard Corp.

Studebaker-Packard Corp. billed itself as America's fourth-largest full-line producer of cars and trucks. The Packard display was among the most interesting. Bodies from 1951-'54 were underneath, but styling was heavily revised. Yet that wasn't the big news: gathering attention was a fresh, big V-8 and the revolutionary Torsion Level Ride, which featured torsion bar suspension (front and back). A working miniature model of the setup was in a case at the display.

Also in the Packard display was the *Request* show car, which featured an early Packard-like grille, and a Patrician four-door sedan that ran 25,000 trouble-free miles at the Packard Proving Grounds at an average speed of 104.737 mph.

Studebaker's revision of its classic 1953-'54 coupes with a chrome-laden grille may have raised questions, but making up for it was the mid-year President Speedster hardtop, which was considered the forerunner of the 1956-and-later Hawks, especially inside.

American Motors Corp.

Nash-Kelvinator Corp. and Hudson Motor Car Co. became American Motors Corp. on May 1, 1954, and Chicago was the first show appearance for the redone 1955 big cars, which now shared the Nash bodies. Ramblers and imported Metropolitans models would now carry Nash and Hudson badges, depending on which dealer group sold them. The company's big cars carried wraparound windshields, and the larger Nash Ambassador and Hudson Hornets were available with new Packard V-8s and Twin Ultramatic transmissions. Sixes from Nash and Hudson roots were also still to be had.

Kaiser-Willys

While the joining of Nash/Hudson and Studebaker/Packard had potential to keep the new corporations going for awhile, such was not the case with Kaiser and its buying of Willys, at least when it came to passenger cars. On display at Chicago for the last time, Kaiser and Willys showed 1955 models, but before the year was over, production in the United States stopped and tooling was shipped to Kaiser in Argentina, where both would enjoy a relatively long life.

Willys tricked up its Aero hardtop and sedan with chrome two-toning and a new Bermuda name for the hardtop. Kaiser continued to show the supercharged Manhattan sedan, which was identical to the 1954 model, probably because it was the same leftover car.

Truck displays

Trucks were mostly separated from cars at the time, unlike today where trucks sometimes dominate displays. Willys Jeeps were among the displays, and the four-wheel-drive vehicles would have a long future at the show.

Chevrolet and GMC had all-new trucks and new V-8 power to brag about. Dodge had added V-8 power to its light-duty lineup in mid-1954 and showed off a test example that did time at the Bonneville Salt Flats and Pike's Peak.

Chicago-based International Harvester had nine trucks on display, ranging from light to heavy duty. Another Chicago firm, Hendrickson, maker of trucks and truck components, was also represented.

Studebaker's trucks reflected new color combinations, and it showed a two-ton chassis on its side to reveal the good stuff underneath. Ford was on hand with its redone 1955 models, which decades later would become some of the most popular restored trucks of the era to restore.

Industry trends in 1955

Besides a color explosion for 1955, it was also the year for widening use of 12-volt ignitions and tubeless tires, air conditioning and power windows, brakes and steering.

If the folks attending the show wanted a break, there were plenty of options. Twice daily, the show's Motorevue was held on the main floor of the center arena. A cast of 75 performers showed off the newest cars from the manufacturers. There was seating for 10,000-12,000 and standing room for more. Community queens, a show tradition, were introduced with the cars. Meanwhile, Ford featured a show of its own by playing a Cinemascope movie featuring its cars, with a special Thunderbird display nearby for those who saw the movie, or could not get in.

In all, the 1955 Chicago Auto Show was a winner. A total of 490,500 visitors passed through the gates in the nine-day run.

CHAPTER 14 | **1955 MERCURY**

By Phil Hall; photos from author's collection

ALMOST ALL-NEW
Clever styling changes and bigger engines made Mercurys modern for '55

Among the Mercurys revised for 1955 was Mercury's lowest-priced model, the Custom two-door sedan. It featured a new grille and bumper, hood, sheet metal, wraparound windshield, taillamps, rear bumper and a 292-cid version of the Y-block V-8. Inside, the instrument panel was redone, as was the trim. The basic body shell used many parts from the 1952-'54 models.

Mercury seemingly tried several schemes to build an identity and escape the lower-priced Ford's shadow since its introduction as a 1939 model. The 1955 models were, perhaps, the most successful effort up to that point, although the cars were still based on bodies shared with Ford, as they had been on the 1952-'54 models.

Mercury production set a record of 329,808 cars for the 1955 model year and was well in line with an industry sales boom, helped by boosting the length of auto loans from two to three years, and a healthy round of styling revisions.

Mercury was not, as claimed, an all-new car for 1955. However, it featured a new Full Scope (wraparound) windshield and revised body panels that were, for the most part, different from Ford. Also new were a revised frame and a longer (by one inch) 119-inch wheelbase and larger brakes. Gone were the non-functional hood scoops from the 1952-'54 models, but the bumper-grille and hooded headlamps of 1955 were attractive and looked truly different than its cousin.

While sedans, wagons and lower-series two-door hardtops shared inner structure pieces with previous models, two new

MERCURY'S NEW MONTCLAIR SERIES

Mercury competitors Oldsmobile and Buick featured new hardtop sedans in 1955, and without its own hardtop four-door, Mercury touted its Montclair as having "hardtop beauty with four-door convenience."

low-roofed two-door hardtops for the new top-of-the-line Montclair line, comprised of a conventional model and a transparent-top Sun Valley, were attention getters. This style was shared with the Ford Crown Victoria and Skyliner version for 1955, but unlike the Fords, the Merc had no center pillar. A mid-year Montclair four-door sedan used the roof, thin door frames and pillars to combat new Oldsmobile and Buick four-door hardtops of 1955.

For the new season, Mercury expanded its market grasp with the Montclair being added to the Monterey and Custom. Series names were simplified from previous years. Montclairs featured a trim piece under the side windows, which adapted well to two-toning when matched to the roof color.

Under the hood, the emerging "horsepower race" was served with a boost from 256 to 292 cubic inches for the Y-Block V-8. Four-barrel carburetors were standard, but it got a bit complicated after that. A 198-hp version with 8.5:1 compression was standard on the Montclair. Standard on the Custom and Montereys with standard three-speed or overdrive transmissions was a 188-hp unit with lower 7.6:1 squeeze.

The 198-hp setup was optional if you had Merc-O-Matic on those two series. Mercury's automatic was also revised for 1955 to offer three speeds instead of two. To reach first gear, there were a couple of paths, as it normally started in second gear (see related story).

Dual exhaust was standard on Montclair, Monterey and Custom wagons. The dual pipes were optional for the rest of the Custom models.

Speaking of the Custom wagon, it was all-steel with no simulated (or real) wood trim, the first Mercury wagon to be so. As a side note, wagons featured Ford rear fenders and taillamp housings, to which revised taillamps were fitted. These taillamps differed from the rest of the line, and from Ford units, and became a popular bolt-on custom addition to Ford coupes and hardtops. Mercury wagons were all eight-passenger units that year with 1954 rear bumpers, while the rest of the line received new bumpers.

In all, there were 10 models to start the season, with Montclair hardtop, Sun Valley hardtop (transparent roof) and convertible. Monterey had a two-door hardtop, four-door sedan and four-door wagon. Custom had the same three body styles as Monterey, but added a price-leader two-door sedan. At mid-year, the Montclair four-door sedan was added. One year later, in mid-year 1956, the Montclair series became the basis for the Phaeton four-door hardtops and the Montclair sedans were dropped.

Since Fords also had the 292-cid V-8, it could be assumed that the larger Mercury was not raced — but it was, although not as intended.

When the GM Hydra-Matic factory burned in 1953, supplies were tight and customer Lincoln decided to look elsewhere for its transmissions and came up with a version of the Borg-Warner-like Ford automatic. Also, the 1955 Lincolns grew longer and heavier from 1954, and it was felt that they could no longer complete successfully in the Carrera Panamerica (Mexican Road Race) as they had in previous years.

Since it was felt that the 1955 Lincolns would not be competitive in the Carrera Panamerica, a group of 1955 Mercury Custom hardtops was built by Bill Stroppe, who prepared the Lincolns. When the race was canceled, Stroppe suggested the Mercurys be raced in AAA stock car events, with modifications. They were entered in AAA events, notably on the paved mile at Milwaukee, with an array of top Indy drivers. Despite the onslaught of Carl Kiekhaefer's Chrysler 300s that season, Stroppe's cars were competitive. Jack McGrath won the last AAA stock car race that year (and forever) in the 200 miler at Milwaukee on Sept. 18. Stroppe returned for 1956 and off and on thereafter in factory-supported Mercurys.

Memories of my fling with a '55 Merc

During high school, this writer spent (and borrowed) way too much money on cars. By graduation time, five vehicles were purchased, ranging from 8 to 2 years old, each time trading in the old one for the next. The lack of frugality and common sense would set a pattern for years to come.

Fourth among the five was a 1955 Mercury Montclair two-door hardtop. A 1953 Chevrolet Bel Air convertible was traded to Burbach De Soto-Plymouth in West Allis, Wis., for the Merc in mid-summer of 1960.

While driving a convertible in high school was good for gaining a number of "friends" who wanted a ride, the old Chevy with Powerglide was just plain slow. A wish for real acceleration when the right pedal was pushed caused the search for some horses, and although it was 5 years old, the 292-cid V-8-powered Mercury seemed like the answer. Being a top-line two-door hardtop also mixed in a "cool" factor.

Features of my "new" 1955 Merc included power steering, brakes and windows. Multi-Luber was new that year and involved a button on the dash and countless fittings underneath to shoot lubrication to various parts. About half of the fittings on my example were disconnected, and pushing the button to show off resulted in a splash of lube oil all over the pavement.

The Montclair was black with white trim, which was duplicated on the inside vinyl interior — with seemingly several square feet of brightwork.

New that year was a three-speed Merc-O-Matic transmission. I was instructed by fellow Mercury drivers that, to get maximum scoot, you started in low, pushed it as far as you could then quickly shifted into drive and back into low, giving you second gear. When that ran out, you went back to drive and made use of all three gears. It worked. My Merc also developed a transmission leak for some reason.

I was very aware of the 198-hp 292 V-8, the top setup that year. Compared to the 1960 cars on the road, it wasn't much, but for this driver, it was something to be used. With others bragging of topping 100 mph in their rigs, it was something I had to try. There were no freeways at the time, so I had to find a stretch of nearby highway that looked long and deserted enough.

Such a location was found and early one Sunday morning I set out to do what must be done. Watching the black-on-white speedometer and

Viewed from its fender skirt-equipped side, the author's 1955 Mercury Montclair was ready for action in the summer of 1960. Being a two-door hardtop, of course all the windows had to be down.

scanning for law enforcement, I made the run and the needle registered 101 mph. It was part of the rites of youth. I was aware that my actual speed may not have been over 100 mph (a lesson from Tom McCahill), but that didn't stop my telling of the deed to all that would listen.

As I said, the cool factor was part of the purchase attraction. In the trunk, I found two rear fender skirts that came with the car and I wondered why they were not installed. It turned out that only one side had the attachment devices. The left rear fender had probably received body work and the devices were left off. Being less than adept at redoing the left side (and having no money), I decided to be half-cool and install just the right skirt. After all, who looks at both sides of the car at the same time?

My one-skirted Montclair carried me down the road for about six months, before trading time came again. One strange feeling during driving it was that it was too much car. I felt all the power equipment was for adults. I liked things simpler...at least at the time.

— Phil Hall

CHAPTER 15 — 1955-'56 CHRYSLER 300
By Pat Olk

FAST TIMES WITH CARL KIEKHAEFER
Early NASCAR owner could run with the best of them

No less than a half dozen Chrysler FirePower Hemi engines were ready to drop in one of Carl Kiekhaefer's racing Chrysler 300s. (John Gunnell collection)

I was 18 and fresh out of high school when I got a job at the Mercury Research Lab, where the Mercury Outboard Racing Team headquarters were located. I worked there through half of the 1955 season and all of 1956.

It seemed they won just about every race they entered during this "stone age of racing."

In 1955, Carl Kiekhaefer raced four 1955 C-300s and one Chevrolet. The Chevrolet was built for one race just to show the factory team that Kiekhaefer could compete with them and beat them. After one winning race, the car was converted back into a company car. The four C-300s were raced in NASCAR and the AAA.

A picture of Kiekhaefer with two cars

Kiekhaefer made quite a showing when he arrived in this convoy of trucks advertising his Mercury outboards and carrying 300s. Tim Flock drove the Chrysler C-300, car No. 300, pictured at the rear of the convoy, and the tank hanging under the truck carrying his car reads, "Flock Juice." (John Gunnell collection)

and drivers Tim Flock and Frank Mundy is especially memorable. The picture was taken at the Oshkosh, Wis., airport using the Kimberly-Clark hangar wall for background. The Mercury Marine hangar was next to it, but Kimberly-Clark's white wall made for a better background.

Kiekhaefer had called the research lab that day because there were some trophies left behind in his office and he wanted them for that picture. He said, "I can get to and from the airport in eight minutes and I expect those trophies here in that time." I rushed the trophies to the airport in a 1955 Chrysler station wagon with a retired 300 racing engine in it. Traffic wasn't as heavy in those days and at one point on Highway 41, I hit 122 mph. The trophies arrived safe and sound in time. Kiekhaefer was happy, and I stayed to watch the photo session.

Kiekhaefer was an extremely intelligent and clever engineer and brought racing into the 20th century. He made many changes in his cars which, at the time, were revolutionary. He had the least amount of bends in the exhaust system of his cars, hence, the knock-out plates under the trunk lid for through-the-trunk exhaust."

Once, while calibrating a '56 Ford engine, he got the idea that longer, straighter exhaust pipes would increase the horsepower. He had his maintenance department knock two concrete blocks out of back wall of the dynamometer room and extend the four-inch pipes out the holes in the wall. The noise reverberated off the steel building 75 feet beyond; it was so loud that the neighbors called the police, who descended on the research lab.

The 1955 Chrysler had two four-inch pipes

Odd as it may seem, the Imperial limousine behind the Daytona Beach Flying Mile-winning Chrysler is relatively important to the history of Kiekhaefer's success: Kiekhaefer had racing tires broke in on the Imperial by driving each set of tires 500 miles before putting them on a race car. (John Gunnell collection)

and the 1956s had four three-inch pipes.

With his dynamometer, Kiekhaefer could break in a new engine and then test it for horsepower. Supposedly, a new 300 engine could only pull about 275 hp. Each of his engines was torn down, rebuilt, honed a secret way, broke in for eight hours on the dynamometer and then calibrated for horsepower.

When a new engine had to be broken in on the dynamometer, it would be done from 10 p.m. to 6 a.m. Two people would stay the night behind the plate glass, operate the counsel and watch the engine. The speed was increased by 500 rpm every two hours. The day crew could then begin calibrating. The engines would be anywhere from 340 to 365 hp when he was done with them. Then, they would be rated, crated and ready for installation.

Kiekhaefer was a fanatic about tires. I think that, up to that time, nobody thought of wide rims. He would cut rims and weld the two wider portions together. The tires were never raced until they had 500 miles on them. To do this, his personal New Yorker and Imperial and other company cars all had racing tires on them. Office personnel would spend their days driving around, putting miles on the tires. After dismounting the tires, Kiekhaefer would personally examine them. Then, they would be balanced and stockpiled for racing. In those days, there were both dirt and asphalt tracks so there were different tires.

One of the ways he intimidated other racing teams was by showing up in the fancy Ford cab-over trucks painted red, white and blue; the cars were all painted white. He had four or five white-uniformed crew members for each car. In those days, cars were driven to the track or towed with a tow bar. There were no trucks or trailers. It was quite a jaw-dropping sight to see his team pull in. To further intimidate everybody, he had stacks and stacks of tires crammed into every space there was in the truck and car. The beautiful leather headliner and side panels were all scuffed black from those tires.

In 1956, he acquired four new Chrysler 300-Bs, two Dodge D-500s and one Dodge D-500 convertible to compete in the new 1956 mid-year convertible circuit with Frank Mundy driving. He also acquired a 1956 Ford, which is a story in itself.

In 1956, AAA disbanded and was replaced by USAC. I think Kiekhaefer just raced NASCAR that year. In 1956, the Ford factory teams were starting to have some success, and Kiekhaefer decided to beat them at their own game. He acquired a "plain Jane" 1956 Mainliner two-door and made a race car out of it. He intended to use it only once, and had a local body shop send out a body man to remove the cloth headliner, to be replaced later.

Ford had a new engine that it was using, and when Kiekhaefer tried to get one, the local Ford dealer told him they didn't exist and weren't listed in the parts book. In those days, if anything was used for racing, it had to be in the parts book and at least 2,000 had to be available for purchase by the general public. "Strictly stock" had to be what was used in race cars, as well as what grandma drove to church on Sunday. It didn't take long for Kiekhaefer to get on the phone to Bill France and any other "powers that be," and he got his parts. He raced once, won and converted the "plain Jane" Ford back again.

Because Kiekhaefer was so successful and always pushing the limit, there seemed to be pending legislation aimed at counteracting his success. Many times, I'd walk by his open office door and hear him jawing at Bill France. He usually always got his way.

As the end of the week approached and race day neared, getting the cars ready became top priority. Employees might punch in at 7 a.m. and still be there the next day at 7 a.m. Kiekhaefer would be right there in his white coveralls working along with everyone else. He had food and refreshments catered in.

Compared to today, in 1955 and 1956, the police were pretty lax. When there was a AAA race at the Milwaukee Mile, the crew would go on Saturday to practice. Instead of trucking the cars down from Oshkosh, they would drive them. They had no mufflers, lights, etc., and would drive right down Highway 41. In Oshkosh, the last thing that was done to a car before race time was to get it aligned. There was a body shop on the other side of town whose owner was trusted by Kiekhaefer to do all of the alignments. He was always on call. An alignment at that time was $7.50 during business hours and $10 any other time. It could be any time of night or early morning when a car would be ready. They would call the

Kiekhaefer raced four Chrysler C-300s and a 1955 Chevrolet in 1955. The Chevrolet is pictured here (far right), and after it won the single race in which it was entered, Kiekhaefer had it converted to a company car. Where did it end up? (John Gunnell collection)

body shop owner and he would be waiting at the shop. The cars would be driven to the shop, again with no mufflers or lights, right through town with a company vehicle in the front and one in the back.

In January 1956, Kiekhaefer acquired a maroon 1956 300-B to race in the Daytona Flying Mile. This was before radar, so to test the speed, they made a speed check unit using two hoses placed so many feet apart. It was similar to what police used in those days. The research plant was situated on an approximate two-mile stretch of road on the northern Oshkosh city limits. One Saturday afternoon, the hoses were set up in front of the building and spotters were placed at each end of the road. When the traffic was clear, the spotters would signal and the car would take off from one end of the road, accelerating as hard and fast as it could reaching speeds over 100 mph as it passed the facility. All this on a city street!

In the fall of 1956, I was hired at a different and better job. I had been a flunky, sweeper and parts chaser with no future at Mercury Marine.

My last day on the job was a Thursday. There was a lot of pre-race activity that week, and lots of night overtime work. Being my last week, I clocked out at 4:30 every day and didn't come back to work at night. That noon, I was by the wash fountain cleaning up for lunch when old man Kiekhaefer spotted me. Unbeknownst to him, this was my last day. He said, "I haven't seen you here at night all week. We have a lot of work to do and I want to see you here tonight. You young guys... all you want to do at night is go out and drink beer!"

Needless to say, I clocked out at 4:30 and never looked back. I think I went out and drank beer that night, too!

CHAPTER 16 / 1956 METROPOLITAN
By Patrick Foster

SEEING DOUBLE
Were there really two different 1956 Metropolitans?

Two second-series 1956 Metropolitans: The coupe is a Nash, while the convertible below is a Hudson. Note the Hudson badge in the grille.

Once in a while, it's difficult to identify what year a particular old car is. You know the problem: there are certain cars, Checker Marathons and VW Bugs, to give just two examples, that changed so little over time that it sometimes takes a bit of ef-

This rare photo shows a first-series 1956 Metropolitan on the showroom floor of Hadsall Nash. The man standing in the center with his suit jacket open is Guy Hadsall. In the lower right corner, you can see a second-series 1956 Met "1500."

fort and expertise to figure out exactly what year a specific car is.

Among the more difficult cars to discern is the Metropolitan, and among Metropolitans, 1956 has to be the most confusing year for model identification. There are two good reasons for that: First, American Motors Corp., which marketed the Met, had a widely misunderstood model year identification policy for all Mets, regardless of year. Second, AMC further muddied the waters by offering two distinctly different series of Mets during 1956.

Let's try to sort this out a bit.

The original Metropolitan was introduced by the Nash Motors division of Nash-Kelvinator in March 1954. Although the car was designed by Nash, to keep the price low, it was manufactured in England by Austin Motor Co. under contract to Nash. The timing of its introduction — coming just weeks before Nash-Kelvinator merged with Hudson Motor Car Co. — meant that almost from the start there would be some confusion, because the car wound end up being sold by both Nash and Hudson deal-

The first-series 1956 Metropolitans had this two-tone paint scheme, no side mouldings. Note the hood's "air scoop."

ers. Although most people think the 1955 Wasp and Hornet were the first Nash-based Hudsons to appear, the first joint product of the merger was actually the 1954 Hudson Metropolitan. Hudson Mets wore Hudson grille badges, while Nash Mets, naturally, wore Nash grille badges. This arrangement continued into 1956, but beginning in 1957, Metropolitan became a separate make within the American Motors family. Rambler also became a separate make that year.

The original Metropolitans had several design touches that were unique to that series. These included an open grille with a single bar running within it and a raised, nonfunctional "air scoop" on the hood. All hardtop coupes came with a two-tone color scheme that included a solid body color and a roof painted Mist Gray — although to most people the Mist Gray color looks like white. Convertibles had a solid body color and a choice of black or tan soft-tops.

All of the early Mets were powered by a 1,200cc Austin-supplied four-cylinder engine, dubbed the A-40. It gave peppy performance and fuel economy of well over 30 mpg — with some owners reporting as much as 40 mpg.

But one confusing aspect of the Metropolitan story is how the company determined a particular car's model year. As expected, dealers ordered cars throughout the year, selling them as current model year cars. But with the change of the model year, which occurred on the day that the new models were introduced, any Metropolitans left in stock automatically became the new models. In other words, a Metropolitan that was ordered by a dealer in early 1955 as a 1955 model automatically became a 1956 model if it was still in stock and unsold as of the announcement day for the 1956 models. They weren't issued new serial numbers or anything like that; it was simply that when they were sold at retail they were registered as the latest model year. Since, initially, the Mets showed very little exterior change, there wasn't any real problem with handling things that way. Dealers weren't stuck with leftover models, and no one had to issue rebates or incentives to move unsold prior-year models, because there simply weren't any! It's an idea I'll bet modern auto makers wish they could copy.

Because the Met's model year was determined by the date of sale rather than by serial number, there are many instances of, say, a 1955 Met having a higher serial number than a 1956 Met. In this case, all that means is that the "1956" probably was originally a 1955 but sat on the dealer lot for a much longer time than the other car. If fate had allowed them both to have been sold on the same day, they both would have been 1955 models; but the 1956 was titled that way because it was sold after the 1956 new car announcement day, when it automatically became a 1956.

Metropolitans sold fairly well in 1954 and 1955, and for 1956 they returned with practically no changes. But confusion began mid-year when AMC introduced a revised and improved Metropolitan. It not only looked substantially different, it was very different mechanically. A number of improvements were introduced, and the Met introduced mid-year 1956 was in many ways a nicer car.

The new Metropolitan had a handsome chrome band surrounding the grille opening, along with a new mesh grille that filled the grille cavity. These two minor revisions gave the Met's frontal appearance a completely new look, more modern and very attractive. The fake air scoop was removed to give the hood a lower, smoother look.

But the biggest change was in the side trim. The Met's body sides, previously unadorned, now wore zigzag moldings which provided the separation for the new standard two-tone paint scheme. On all hardtop Mets, the roof was now painted Snowberry White, which didn't look all that much different from before, but now the roof color was also used on the lower body sides. The primary paint color was only on those areas of the body above the side moldings and below the roof. Convertibles also were given this color scheme, with soft-tops offered only in black. There were numerous mechanical changes as well. The new series was powered by the Austin A-50 four-cylinder engine, a 1,500cc unit good for 52 hp and 77 lb.-ft. of torque, versus 42 hp and 62 lb.-ft. of torque on the earlier Mets. The new engine provided greatly improved acceleration, a higher top speed and, interestingly, better fuel economy!

There were other changes in the new Mets, but the main point is that the exterior appearance of this new car was quite different from the previous Metropolitans, and mechanically they were different, too. The new series entered production at the beginning of the calendar year and began showing up on dealer lots during the spring. That presented a problem, because although they were being introduced mid-year, for some reason American Motors didn't choose to call them early 1957s. And because the foundation of the Met's model identification was that cars in stock were always of the current model year, until such time as the next model year cars debuted, that meant that AMC would be marketing two distinctly different cars as 1956 Metropolitans.

Confusing? Definitely!

Luckily, Carl Chakmakian of AMC's Product Planning and Information department came up with a viable solution. He suggested calling the new series the Metropolitan "1500," a name taken from the new car's engine size in cubic centimeters. It would provide a degree of separation in the minds of buyers, and, besides, it was common enough practice among import cars back then to include some sort of reference to engine size, and usually it was expressed just this way, rounded off to the nearest "cc."

Very Continental.

So Metropolitan "1500" it was. The older vehicles in stock were belatedly referred to as the Metropolitan "1200" series, though no such badges were ever attached to the cars. It just made it easier during conversations to use the "1200" and "1500" designations rather than getting into a lengthier description. The two models were often sold side by side in showrooms, at least until the earlier models were sold out.

All this means that if you see a Metropolitan described as a 1956, but it has the 1,200cc engine and the earlier color scheme, don't automatically dismiss it as a mistake. Many people believe that all 1956 Metropolitans should have the zigzag side trim and mesh grille, but that's not the case. Thousands of first-series (1,200cc) Mets were sold as 1956 models, and they're correct. In fact, I wouldn't be surprised if there were a few 1955 or 1956 1,200cc Mets that ended up being sold even later and registered as 1957s. After all, although Mets were hot in California and New York, in certain markets, Metropolitans were not big sellers, places like Minnesota and North Dakota, for example. So it should come as no surprise if they sat a while before being sold.

But no matter how long it took to sell them, at least we know those Mets were always the latest model year; they couldn't be anything but!

CHAPTER 17 | **1956 STUDEBAKER TRUCK**
By Phil Hall

CIVILIZING THE TRUCK
Adding creature comforts to the 1956 Studebaker pickup

Radical — for Studebaker — two-tone paint was optional for the 1956 model Transtar trucks from South Bend. A revised grille and new hood scoop also marked the models that year, which were altered in reaction to the changing marketplace. The rain and sun visors over the windows in the doors were standard equipment. (Phil Hall collection)

In the grand scheme of the American truck's transition from work vehicle to personal transportation, the mid to late 1950s could be considered the early roots of the revolution. While the ruggedness of the light-duty pickup wasn't especially compromised during the period, exterior and interior styling was enhanced to appeal to the style-conscious buyer that previously had considered only passenger cars.

Perhaps the first solid example of this trend was the second-series 1955 Chevrolet Cameo Carrier, which featured flush fiberglass sides to the standard bed, complete with chrome and two-toning.

Upgraded interiors, wraparound windshields and smoother body lines all were worked into the domestic light-duty pickups in the middle 1950s. Ford introduced an all-new body for 1953 (and would get another for 1957), Dodge was restyled for 1954 and was fitted with a wrapped windshield in mid 1955 and the same year, there were radically new Chevrolet and GMC trucks.

All of this put pressure on the independent manufacturer Studebaker, which had a small-but-consistent following in the truck field. The last all-new Studebaker pickup was the 1949 2R, which was modern for the time, but was increasingly dated by mid-decade. Even though Studebaker merged with Packard to form Studebaker-Packard Corp. in 1955, cash for a truck redesign was not realistic. The restyled 1956 Studebaker passenger cars, including the Hawk series, took most of what funds there were.

As a result, Studebaker trucks for 1956 were physically much the same as previous models. However, that doesn't mean that the demands of the market were lost on the folks in South Bend, Ind.

Featured in the 1956 2E trucks were subtle changes that held a few milestones for Studebaker fans. They were named "Transtar" and carried badges on the doors to proclaim the name. Optional was two-tone paint that carried from the bed to a sweep in the middle of the door. No chrome trim, no trick bodywork, just paint. It detracted some attention from the old flared-fender bed that, like the cab, dated to 1949. It came in 6-1/2- and 8-foot lengths.

Studebaker two-tone paint bowed during the 1955 model run. Also held over from 1955 was the basic grille. At the end of the lower ribs were new stylized directional signal/parking lights. However, the old ones under the headlights also came along for the ride.

The hood was redesigned with a new scoop/vent in the leading edge. Lettering spelled out "Studebaker" across the middle.

The rain and sun visors over the doors, which looked like add-on accessories, were continued as standard equipment for 1956.

New inside was the first Deluxe Cab option. Instead of the dull basic trim, a Saran-covered seat with foam rubber lining added comfort. An insulated acoustic headliner replaced cardboard. Unfortunately, armrests disappeared.

For power, the half-ton line came with a choice of a newly enlarged 185.5-cid flathead six out of the Champion, or 224.3-cid V-8, which was no longer available in the passenger cars. The trucks also received 12-volt systems for 1956, following the trend of the industry.

Stude trucks had several transmission options to the three-speed standard unit. Overdrive and four-speed manual transmissions could be had on both engines, and a three-speed automatic was available for V-8-powered trucks. Standard transmission units could also be had with Studebaker's famed Hill-Holder, which applied brakes when the clutch was pushed in.

All of this in a vacuum would have been impressive, but the competition had most of it and more, with more modern styling. Even International would be all-new during 1957.

Sales dropped from 1955, when the Studebaker pickups first saw V-8 power.

For 1957, a new fiberglass front grille surround and more radical trim actually made the Transtars look different. However, sales continued to slide as Studebaker progressed to its eventual truck demise in late 1963. Even a low-buck Scotsman for 1958 and Lark-based Champ for 1959 wouldn't help.

Much of what gussied up for 1956 was still around on the final 1-ton 1964 model pickups.

CHAPTER 18 — **1956-'57 EL MOROCCO**

Story and photos by Bill Siuru

1956-'57 EL MOROCCO
No longer a poor man's Eldorado

For both El Morocco years, the stock Chevrolet grilles were rearranged and modified to better resemble the respective Cadillac models.

I've heard of them, but never saw one in person until I got to see two up close at the recent Heartbeat Classic Chevy Car Show in Valley Center, Calif. Since there were two El Morocco convertibles, it was easy to see the differences between the 1956 and 1957 versions, the only two years they were offered.

77

These El Moroccos can most likely be mistaken for Eldorados when viewed from the rear.

The El Morocco was created by millionaire Reuben Allender, a Canadian who came to Detroit and made a fortune in several enterprises, including selling World War II surplus textiles. A long-time Cadillac owner, he bought a 1955 Eldorado and realized that the "tri-five" Chevrolets could be customized to look like the Cadillac Eldorados. The 1956 El Morocco resembled the 1955-'56 Eldorado convertibles and 1956 Eldorado Seville hardtop, while the 1957 model mocked the Eldorado Brougham introduced in 1957.

Most of the credit for executing Allender's ideas goes to tool-and-die maker Robert Thompson. Fiberglass work was done by Creative Industries in Detroit and master fiberglass fabricator Cyril Olbrich. Metal trim parts that weren't from other cars were fabricated by Wettlaufer Engineering, also in Detroit. Allender purchased cars to be modified from Don McCoullagh Chevrolet in Detroit.

Modifications were strictly cosmetic; the mechanics and interiors were kept stock. The model was named El Morocco, after a famous New York City nightspot.

Body reworking was mostly at the rear. For the 1956 model, rear fenders were cut off and replaced with fiberglass tail fins blended into the rear quarter panels with epoxy resin. Tail fins on the 1957 El Morocco were steel and welded on. After the original trim was removed, holes were leaded in. While the rear bumper on the '56 El Moroccos was stock Chevy, the one on the '57 was unique and done by Wettlaufer Engineering.

Allender used some parts from the big automaker's parts bins. The twin bullet taillamps on the 1956 model came from the 1955-'56 Dodge, but turned 90 degrees. The tail lamp inserts on the 1957 version were donated by the 1956 Plymouth. Reportedly, the huge "Dagmars" on the '56's front bumpers were made from headlamp buckets from the 1937 Dodge, but turned around and chromed. The rear ones on the '57 came from the 1954 Mercury. The Sabre-spoke wheels were like ones in the J.C. Whitney catalog.

While there are conflicting production figures, there were probably no more than 30 in the two years of production. About half were convertibles, the rest were two- and four-door hardtops. As might be expected, four-doors were only made in 1957, because the 1957 Eldorado Brougham was a four-door. While the ragtops were Bel Airs, the only trim level for convertibles in 1956-'57, Two-Tens were used for the two- and four-doors.

Contrary to common legend, the El Moroccos were never an official GM product sold by Chevrolet dealers with a GM-backed warranty, though Allender did initially hope to get Chevrolet dealers to put them in their showrooms. Apparently, they were only available through Allender & Co. in Detroit, and the warranty issue was a bit nebulous. Also, GM never requested Allender to cease building the El Morocco. In fact, GM barely knew that Allender was building it. Depending on the state, they were titled as Chevrolets, Chevrolet customs, or even El Moroccos.

At prices ranging from $2,750 to $3,250, El Moroccos were only about $600 to $800

Allender and his group did a very creditable job of making the El Morocco (above top) mimic the real Eldorado (above).

more than the corresponding Chevrolet models. This was far less than the $6,500 for a 1956 Eldorado Biarritz or $13,000 for a 1957 Eldorado Brougham. Considering the work involved in the conversion and the few sold, this was not a money maker for Allender. Thus, there was no 1958 model. Besides, the major changes in the 1958 Chevrolets would have made the modifications significantly more difficult.

CHAPTER 19 | **1956-'57 LINCOLNS**
By Phil Hall

BIGGER *WAS* BETTER
Bigger 1956 and '57 Lincolns stood tall against competition

The only way to photograph a hardtop is with the windows down. Lincoln got it right when it photographed its first four-door hardtop, which arrived in 1957.

A classic example of the "longer, lower, wider" syndrome of the 1950s can be found in the 1956 Lincoln. The all-new luxury car grew 7.3 inches in length, dropped 2.5 inches in height and expanded 2.3 inches in width over the 1955 models. Since the wheelbase grew from 123 to 126 inches, that extra length (and then some) was added to the rear overhang.

Mechanix Illustrated's famed scribe Tom McCahill noted the new Lincoln had more rear overhang "than an 1855 China Tea Clipper."

Nautical comparisons aside, the mid-1950s luxury field was full of barges (sorry about that). Cadillac and Packard were in that class and Imperial, which went on its own for 1955, was hefty, too. Meanwhile, Lincoln for 1955 stayed with its 1952-'54 design (including the non-wraparound windshield), stressing handling and its three victories in the Pan American Road Race.

81

✳ LINCOLN

The Lincoln Premiere Coupe

People who know fine cars are changing to Lincoln

More fine car buyers are changing to Lincoln this year than ever before in Lincoln's entire history — because they recognize that this longest, lowest, most powerful Lincoln of all time is unmistakably . . . the finest in the fine car field.

Naturally, most of these discriminating buyers are turning to Lincoln because of its fresh, trend-setting new styling. But after *owning* Lincoln, they praise this car's other fine qualities.

They tell us — time and time again — about Lincoln's exceptional handling ease. They're surprised that such a big, roomy car can be so effortless to drive — and that wives prefer this Lincoln over the family's smaller car . . . because it's easier to handle, and as easy to park.

They tell us, too, about Lincoln's outstanding performance — in dozens of ways. Those who experience Turbo-Drive for the first time are astonished to find that an automatic transmission can be so smooth . . . and those who take long trips say that this Lincoln makes the ride seem so much shorter — and so free of fatigue.

And as you might expect, we also hear about Lincoln's superb roadability. Owners like the way this big car rides so firmly through a curve — and the freedom of taking any road they choose . . . instead of avoiding the bad ones.

Obviously, we could tell you about this enthusiasm at great length. But if you've been thinking this is *your* kind of fine car, it's time you stopped in to see your Lincoln dealer.

Lincoln stressed size and luxury in its ads for the all-new 1956 models. Also in the copy was mention of handling characteristics, for which its 1952-'55 models were famous. This ad showed off the Premiere Coupe.

82

It joined the big boys' club for 1956, not only getting a wraparound windshield, but also truly new styling. At the top of the line was the new Premiere series, comprised of convertible, two-door hardtop and six-window four-door sedan. A step down was the Capri nameplate, which used to be the top wrung. Two-door hardtops and four-door sedans resided here.

While Lincoln was the only all-new domestic standard segment luxury car for 1956, it was overshadowed by the ultra-luxury Continental Mark II from Ford Motor Co. While many associated the new Continental with Lincoln, due to the first 1940-'48 Continentals being branded such, the new $10,000 offering did not carry a Lincoln nameplate. Technically, the car came from the short-lived Continental Division. The Continental Mark II did not match sales predictions and, after a run of unchanged 1957 models, it disappeared. The Continental name returned to the Lincoln fold starting with the 1958 models, but that is another story.

Lincoln had a styling story to tell for 1956, but it had a heritage of being a fine-handling luxury car, thanks to the 1952-'55 models, and made an effort to tell prospective buyers it still could go around corners. With a heavier frame, the 1956 Lincoln retained coil springs with ball joints up front and leaf springs in the rear, but the 200 lbs. of added heft opened questions of how good it was.

McCahill, who owned and bragged about the handling of his 1953 Lincoln, got an early crack at the 1956 and brought along a 1955 Lincoln for comparison.

"Any grade school student of physics could quickly tell these changes are bound to alter Lincoln's handling characteristics," he said of the size and weight additions.

After wringing out both the 1955 and 1956 offerings, he concluded "the engineers, in spite of my skepticism, had maintained the cornering qualities of the car."

Also helping appeal and a must in the midst of the "horsepower race," Lincoln enlarged its V-8 from 341 to 368 cubic inches and its advertised horsepower from 225 to 285 units. It came attached to its upgraded Turbo-Drive automatic transmission.

Despite being an off year in sales, the 1956 Lincoln was a success. The model run of 50,322 was the second-best ever, and a big jump over the 1955 tally of 27,222 cars.

Lincoln hoped to continue the momentum with its face-lifted 1957 models. In hindsight, they did not have the styling appeal of the 1956 models. The cars featured huge fins, or "canted blades," as the literature referred to them. Up front, the modified 1956 grille featured "Quadra-Lites," which were an early form of quad headlights. The top lights were standard 7-inch units, while the lowers were 5 3/4-inch units that, at first, were considered driving lights, until the quad setup was legalized in all states.

Lincoln Premiere Two-Door Hardtop

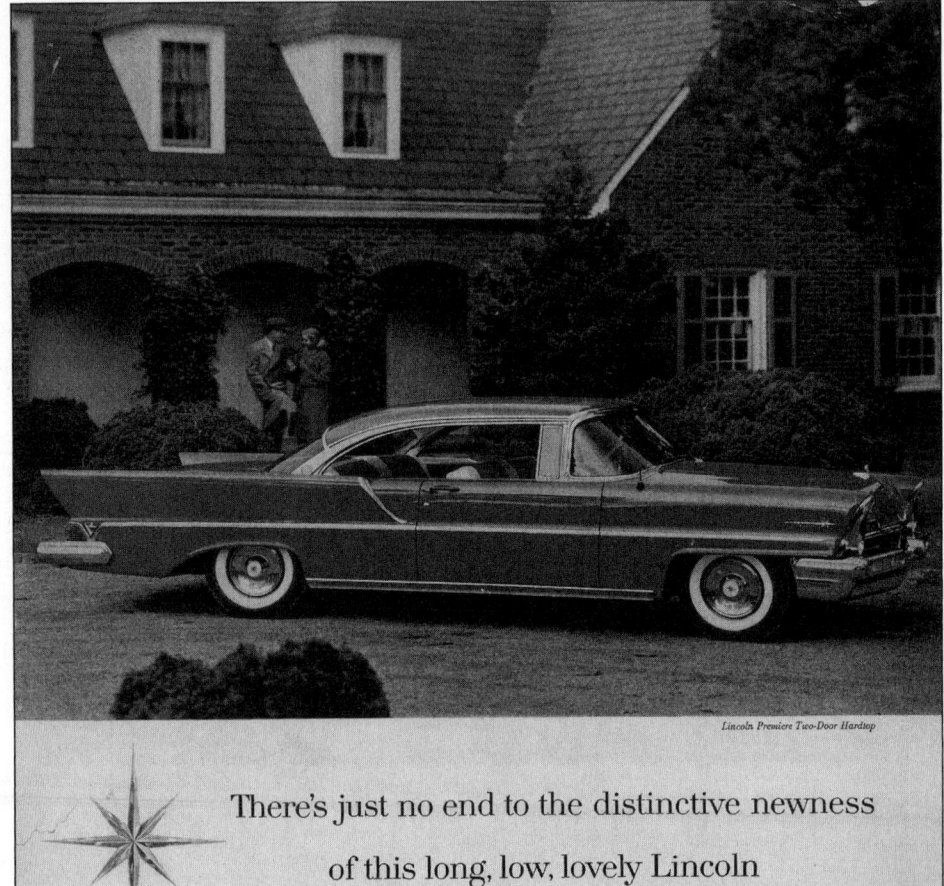

There's just no end to the distinctive newness of this long, low, lovely Lincoln

First you see dramatic new beauty, from distinctive Quadra-Lite Grille to crisp, canted rear blades. Then, every mile you drive brings a new revelation of handling ease that's uniquely, wonderfully Lincoln's. The newness, you'll find, never ends, and that's why more and more fine car owners are changing to this finest Lincoln ever.

From the first moment you relax behind the wheel, you find how magnificently Lincoln's crisp, new styling fulfills itself—in action.

No other fine car is so effortless to drive. The most complete array of important power luxuries in any car brings a new, easy mastery to every driving situation. A new, fast-action Turbo-Drive transmission puts this most powerful Lincoln of all time instantly and smoothly at your command . . . in every speed range.

And Lincoln's exclusive new Hydro-Cushion suspension system smooths out the roughest roads . . . relaxes you along your way as no other car can. Indeed, many a new Lincoln owner tells us with astonishment that the longest day's journey leaves him with no driving fatigue whatsoever.

See all this exciting newness at your Lincoln dealer's—drive it where you will. Then and only then will you know why the trend among discerning fine car buyers is unmistakably to Lincoln.

LINCOLN DIVISION, FORD MOTOR COMPANY

LINCOLN
Unmistakably . . . the finest in the fine car field

1957

"Long, low and changed" this 1957 Lincoln ad proclaimed. The Quadra-Lite grille and "canted rear blades" (fins to the rest of us) were highlighted on this Premiere two-door hardtop. "Unmistakably...the finest in the fine car field" the ad bragged.

A cheerful model shows off Lincoln's long, low and beautiful 1957 convertible.

Also new was Lincoln's first four-door hardtop, labeled a "Landau." It was available in both the Premiere and Capri series.

A boost from a 9:1 to 10:1 compression ratio and a new four-barrel carburetor were good for a boost to 300-advertised horsepower. Engine size remained the same at 368 cubes. There was a bit more mass to haul, as length grew to 224.5 inches from 222.9 and width edged from 79.9 to 80.3 inches, which put the 1957 Lincoln over the legal limit for passenger cars in some states.

Despite the changes, production fell to 41,193, but it wasn't entirely the fault of the 1957 changes for Lincoln. Both Cadillac and Imperial were all new with the latter of a spectacular persuasion. On the other side of the coin, Packard left the segment with the name attached to Studebakers for 1957 and 1958.

From a collector standpoint, the 1956 Lincoln, model for model, outranks the values of the 1952-'55 predecessors. The 1957s are also priced a shade under the 1956 examples. However, the 1956-'57 models would be appreciated even more after production stopped. The radically styled, unitized, all-new 1958 Lincolns and the 1959-'60 models that followed would become an acquired taste. They, too, fall behind the 1956-'57s in collector value.

Lincoln changed course again with its totally new 1961 models, but that, too, is another story.

CHAPTER 20 | **1957 CHEVROLET BEL AIR**

Story and photos by Jim Bauer

HEAVEN IN A '57
Chevy love affair survives 46 years and cross-country moves

The author bought his beloved 1957 Bel Air in 1963, but didn't complete its restoration back to showroom condition until 2008.

I was 18 years old and working at Ray's Texaco in San Mateo, Calif., when I first started attending to Mrs. Pierce's 1957 Chevrolet Bel Air Sport Coupe. Mrs. Pierce was a customer of Ray's Texaco, and I saw that car there while working at the station in high school and college. It was at Ray's that I developed my love and knowledge of cars, especially Mrs. Pierce's Chevy.

Mrs. Pierce bought the car at Ernest Ingold-George Olsen Chevrolet at 999 Van Ness in San Francisco on July 17, 1957.

Six years later, Mrs. Pierce returned to the Chevy dealership to trade her 1957 Chevy for a new 1963 Impala; she was going to receive $650 from the dealership for the '57 Chevy. Not being bashful, I asked Mrs. Pierce if she would sell the '57 to me for $650. She agreed after some thought, then she and I went down to the California DMV together. I gave her the $650 and she signed the title over to me. This was in the days when you knew the customers that came into your station, asked how they were and you provided them with a service.

After I graduated from college, I lost my II-S draft status and became, as they say, "1A" and went off to serve in the Vietnam conflict. I left my beloved '57 with my mother, and she drove it until she passed away.

When I returned from Vietnam, I married, started having kids and forgot about the '57, which sat in my parents' garage in San Mateo, Calif., until 1977. At that time, I retrieved it from San Mateo and drove it to Los Gatos, Calif. When I was transferred to Reno, Nev., I took the '57 with me. The next move was to Sacramento, and again, the '57 came along. The next big move was to Carlisle, Pa., where it was transported in a moving van and then left to sit in a barn.

By the late 1990s, I was ready to get serious about restoring the Chevy. The body-off-frame rebuild was started by Carlisle Customs and Classics in the late '90s, but then I was transferred to south Florida. The car then sat in Carlisle with the chassis and drive train rebuilt, the body work completed and the parts painted with the doors and trunk mounted, but everything else was in boxes. Even the front fenders and hood were painted, but were stacked throughout the shop. In 2005, I became very sick and told the shop to stop all work on the '57.

After retiring in January 2008 from IBM (we joke the company's initials stand for "I've Been Moved"), I became serious about finishing the restoration. My youngest son and I flew to Harrisburg, Pa., and rented a 20-foot truck and trailer and drove to Carlisle. We packed the truck with boxes of new and old parts, loaded the '57 on the trailer and hauled it all back to Weston, Fla., in August 2008. I found my old assembly manual and proceeded to re-assemble it. I had help putting all new glass back in the car, but my son and I did everything from wiring, putting the interior together, getting it started and running and finally hanging the fenders hood, bumpers, etc.

For me and my car, it has been a 47-year love affair.

'50s Flashback: Features of the fabulous '57s

Though its body was essentially the same one introduced in 1955, the '57 Chevrolet looked brighter, more modern and larger than the 1955 and 1956 models. Traditional-size 1957 Chevys from all three series (base One-Fifty, mid-level Two-Ten and top-of-the-line Bel Air models) also had much sharper rear edges to the rear fenders, which have become a symbol of the period.

A Chevrolet medallion was set into a center cavity within a new horizontal grille bar, floating in a front bumper design integrated into the front sheet metal. Windsplit bulges ran along both sides of the flat hood panel. They were decorated in front with bombsight ornaments. The hooded headlamps were set into small grilles housed in square-looking fender openings. There were screens above the headlamps.

While the base 1957 One-Fifty models were trimmed much the same as the 1955 Two-Ten and Bel Air models, the '57 Two-Ten models were upgraded with double body-side moldings on the rear quarters and were available with contrasting paint between them. Bel Airs had an even richer look with silver anodized insert panels between the twin moldings, gold grille highlights and extra trim, including gold front fender chevrons to match the hood and trunk lid emblems.

Chevrolet listed triple-locking door latches and "High-Volume Ventilation" as new selling features. One six-cylinder, the 235.5-cid with 140 hp, served as the base powerplant in all series, and cars powered as such featured a large Chevrolet crest on the hood and trunk. Regardless of which V-8 powerplant was under the hood, Chevrolets with eight-cylinder power featured a "V" and "Chevrolet" emblem on both the hood and trunk. The smallest V-8 was painted chartreuse and displaced 265 cubic inches; this engine is believed to have been offered only in the beginning of the model year. The remaining six V-8s in 1957 displaced 283 cubic inches with various fuel-delivery systems, from a single two barrel carburetor (185 hp) to a single four-barrel (220 hp) to a pair of dual four-barrel engines (245 or 270 hp) to a pair of fuel-injected 283s (250 or 283 hp). A three-speed manual transmission, available with overdrive at extra cost, and Powerglide or Turboglide automatics were offered.

The Bel Air Sport Coupe (two-door hardtop) featured here represents one of the most popular cars among collectors today; it falls just behind the convertible and nearly even with the sporty two-door Nomad station wagon among the most popular icons of the "finned '50s."

CHAPTER 21 | **1957 NASH**

By James Mays

END OF THE LINE

Nash's journey ended with '57 models

The 1957 Nash Ambassador Custom two-door hardtop was the company's top-of-the-line model, but it wasn't a good seller. Even advertising showing people in suits and furs wasn't enough to convince the public that the Nash was a status-symbol car.

Folks from Maine to Alaska and Florida to Hawaii got their first peek at the 1957 Nash Ambassador on Oct. 25, 1956. Once they got into the show rooms, consumers were treated to a radically changed senior Nash, billed this year as the "world's newest and finest travel car." Gone was the lower-priced, slow-selling Statesman. Gone were all six-cylinder models. Every big Nash was an Ambassador dressed in Super or upscale Custom trim. The top-of-the-line models wore Country Club badges and were even more refined.

Although the basic body shell had not been changed since 1955 (some will argue 1952), the facelift achieved by the stylists was quite effective. Those inboard headlamps — a European trait inspired by the Nash-Healey — had migrated from the large oval grille back to the more traditional position on the fenders. If that wasn't change enough, voila, they were doubled to create stacked quad lamps — an industry first — one proudly shared with another luxury make. Fenders were capped with turn signals sheathed in chrome spears.

A massive ovoid grille was filled with a tightly knit tartan-weave pattern, double-edged in chrome. At the center of the grille rode the proud Nash emblem, underscored by an unmistakable gold "V." The stand-up hood ornament mounted on the prow was distinguished: twin jets sharing a chrome band, poised in flight. Another distinctive

89

touch was the slightly recessed hood that permitted the cowl intake of fresh air, yet another hallmark of Nash Motors' independent thinking and superior design.

For the first time since the 1949 models, the front wheel wells were opened fully. That dropped the turning circle from 45 feet, 10 inches to a more modest 42 feet, even though the car still rode on a 121.3-inch wheelbase and measured 209.3 inches in length — without the installation of the optional continental spare. Wheels themselves were downsized to 14 inches.

The flanks of the envelope were slab-sided with the more expensive models carrying Z-streak or "lightning streak" chrome trim that lent itself perfectly to optional two-tone and tri-tone paint applications. Although it did not sport fins like many of the competing cars, designers had subtly opened up the lines at the top of the belt line above the rear wheel well to create a generous and powerful fuselage look in the hind quarters.

Despite the fact that the roof line had been carefully chopped by a full 2 inches, the greenhouse was vast. It was cleverly set off with a Euro-look indent that framed the door tops, making the car look dramatically lower than it actually was. Nash carried a wraparound windshield and could boast it was the largest one in the industry. At the rear, huge lollipop tail lamps rode atop long-stemmed, extra-cost back-up lamps. Another popular extra-cost item was the continental spare that looked particularly at home on the large Nash and gave the Travel King added sophistication and pizzazz.

In April of 1956, American Motors Corp. had dropped the Packard-sourced V-8 engine and — with great fanfare — introduced a V-8 of its own design. The thin-wall cast engine measured 327 cubic inches and used the most modern technology the world had to offer. Created in-house by AMC's engineer David Potter, the 255-hp mill was a thing of joy. Prospective customers were invited to "step on the throttle and — get that feel of surging power — unbelievable smooth power." Gone was the extra-cost Packard Twin-Ultramatic transmission; the new corporate mill was mated to GM's more reliable Hydra-Matic shifter.

With color schemes and materials chosen by the famed Helene Rothier, Nash interiors were as sumptuous as interiors could possibly be. All were dressed in luxurious vinyls, fabrics and leathers. For the fifth year in a row, Nash could rightfully claim its passengers rode in the largest and widest cabins in the industry. Six football fullbacks could ride all day in the roomy Nash, seated on firm, supportive cushions, and not experience the least bit of road fatigue. Front seats folded flat to create Twin-Travel Beds — turning any Nash into a convenient roadside Hilton. The extra-cost All-Season Air made travel most pleasurable, as heater and air-conditioning were available in a single unit.

The instrument panel was as wide as the open prairie and made use of an attractive engine-turned overlay to set a dignified and posh tone for the driver. The instrument cluster was mounted in the center of the panel. A large speedometer containing gauges and idiot lamps was to the left, while radio and heater controls were found in the middle and the clock to the right. Duo-Coustic speakers flanked the panel at the ends. Always different from its competitors, the expansive Nash glove box was mounted in the center of the panel, beneath the heat and air conditioning controls. The classy storage compartment didn't merely open, it slid in and out — like a drawer — on ball bearings.

Options for one's Nash Ambassador were as plentiful as clover in a summer field. They included such niceties as power steering, power brakes, power-lift windows, windshield washers, a radio, the Airliner seats that reclined to make the Twin-Travel Beds, the fabled Weather Eye heater and defroster and the All-Season Air Conditioner with Solex glass. One could order an electric clock, leather seat trim, padded sun visors, seat belts and the continental-mounted spare. Back-O-Matic lamps were useful, as was an oil filter and an oil-bath air cleaner.

Despite two-tone and tri-tone color schemes in 32 hues — 15 of them new for 1957 — people didn't rush to buy the natty Nash. Advertising did its best, using models decked out in tuxedoes and evening gowns to give the Nash added status. Unfortunately, the times were changing, and the public was no longer enamored with big cars.

The grand name would be laid to rest with the last Nash rolling off the line in June of 1957. After 40 years, the name had outlived its usefulness. The Nash legacy and heritage would live on in the spirit of the Rambler, a car that captured the public's imagination.

CHAPTER 22 | 1957 PLYMOUTH
By John Lee

UNCOVERING THE BURIED BELVEDERE
An event 50 years in the making

The day the Belvedere was buried. Who could have guessed then that the finned fantasy would be old-fashioned in just a few years? (Tulsa Historical Society, Bud and Walter Brewer Collection)

Someone with ties to Tulsa, your new Plymouth is about to be delivered!

Whadaya mean? They don't even make Plymouths anymore!

Well, sir or madam, we're talking about a brand-new 1957 Plymouth Belvedere Sport Coupe. So where's it been for the last 50 years? Buried in a time capsule underneath the lawn of the Tulsa, Okla., County Courthouse.

It seems that back when the 1957 Plymouth was adorning a Tulsa dealer's showroom, Oklahoma was celebrating the 50th anniversary of the year Indian Territory became the new state of Oklahoma. Oklahoma City, the state capital, apparently had a lot of celebratory activities going on, which rival Tulsans considered a challenge to come up with something that would gain more attention.

The result was Tulsa's week-long observance of the Oklahoma Golden Jubilee, capped off by sealing memorabilia of the day into a time capsule and burying it underneath the Tulsa County Courthouse lawn. The ceremony took place on June 15, 1957, with the sealed vault to be opened 50 years later.

Hey, that's June 15, 2007!

But this is Tulsa. The traditional tin box with a letter from the mayor, some coins, the day's newspaper and other souvenirs just wouldn't do. The Jubilee Committee decided the most suitable representation of 1957 civilization would be — a new car!

"This is the sort of thing that could happen only in Tulsa," Lewis Roberts Jr., Tulsa event chairman, proclaimed during dedication ceremonies as citizens prepared to entomb a new 1957 Plymouth Belvedere Sport Coupe.

Why a Plymouth Belvedere? The official line, according to Jubilee Chairman W.A. Anderson, was, "In our judgment, Plymouth is a true representative of automobiles of this century, with the kind of lasting appeal that should still be in style 50 years from now." So much for clairvoyance. Little did Anderson or anyone else know that Chrysler Corp.'s Forward Look would be passé four years later — the fins, rakish forward-thrusting front fenders and flashy two-tone treatments would be a thing of the past. And who could have imagined that the rock-solid Plymouth nameplate would disappear entirely from the automotive scene before 2007!

Did the Jubilee Committee actually choose the Plymouth, or were the Plymouth dealers just the first to offer a free car for the promotion? Very likely, it was a combination of those factors, and possibly others.

The choice must have appeared to be a good one at the time. Plymouth's all-new styling for 1957, advertised with a "Suddenly it's 1960!" theme, was the most modern of the low-priced three. The comparable Ford model, the Fairlane 500 hardtop, was also new and modern, with plenty of glass, canted rear fender fins and large, round taillamps resembling rocket exhausts. Lots of new bright trim lent flash to the new Chevrolet Bel Air, but the rather squarish, slab-sided styling was a face lift of a three-year-old design.

Not that any of these three designs would have the "lasting appeal that should still be in style 50 years from now," but certainly

Crane operators, police officers and construction workers were all part of automotive history on June 15, 1957. (Tulsa Historical Society, Bud and Walter Brewer Collection)

hindsight would reveal that the iconic Bel Air would have better represented 1957 50 years later. Styling aside, however, the 1957 Belvedere was as modern as any, with a well-engineered OHV V-8 engine, new push-button-operated three-speed automatic transmission and acclaimed torsion-bar suspension.

The Plymouth Division of Chrysler Corp. cooperated with Tulsa Plymouth dealers Wilkerson Motor Co., Cox Motor Co., Vance Motor Co., Forster Riggs and Parrish-Clark to supply the Belvedere for the promotion. Several items were entombed along with the car: a 5-gallon can of gasoline (in case that fuel was no longer in use in 2007), a jar of Oklahoma crude oil and an unpaid parking ticket.

The glove box holds the typical contents of a lady's purse: 14 bobby pins, a compact plastic rain cap, several combs, a tube of lipstick, pack of gum, facial tissues, $2.73 in bills and coins, a pack of cigarettes with matches and a bottle of tranquilizers.

As part of the Golden Jubilee festivities, citizens were invited to guess what Tulsa's population would be in the year 2007. The guesses were then recorded on microfilm and sealed in a steel container buried with the car. When the car and artifacts are excavated, the person whose guess is closest to Tulsa's 2007 population is to be awarded the Belvedere. If that person is dead, the car is to be awarded to his or her heirs.

The "current population" figure for purposes of awarding the car will be determined by consulting the U.S. Census Bureau for its estimate on June 1. According to Bob Ball of the Tulsa Metro Chamber of Commerce, the city's 2006 population estimate was 388,125. The Tulsa population was 261,616 in 1957.

Ron Blissit confirmed that the buried Belvedere did have a V-8, probably the "optional" 299.6-cid version that somehow came to be termed the 301. With a 8.5:1 compression ratio and standard two-barrel carburetor, this engine was rated at 215 hp. It could have been fitted with a four-barrel carb ($39) and dual exhausts ($19.80), equipment that would boost the power rating to 235 hp. Plymouth sold 67,268 Belvedere Sport Coupes in 1957.

At the time, Blissit was a high school senior working after school and Saturdays at the Forster Riggs dealership, where his dad was the general manager. As he recalled, the new Belvedere hardtop was brought over from the Parish-Clark agency, and he helped ready it for burial. "I don't remember what all we did," he said, but he did remember the engine being covered with plastic. Supposedly, the Plymouth was coated with cosmoline or a similar metal-preserving substance, and some accounts say the entire car was wrapped in plastic. The gold-and-white hardtop is sitting on a steel skid and enclosed within a concrete bunker. A bronze plaque on the courthouse sidewalk marks its location.

Blissit knew the man who sprayed a gunite water barrier onto the concrete vault. Some fear vibrations from years of heavy traffic going by only 15 or 20 feet away might have caused the vault to crack. As for maintenance, a building operations staff member quipped, "We just cut the grass on top of it!"

The 1957 event didn't get Blissit too excited. He was not overly impressed with the 1957 Plymouth, although his mother drove one. He was enjoying the power of a 1956 Dodge D-500.

"I thought they were kidding," said Blissit, of first hearing about the Plymouth burial. He was at work and didn't witness the ceremony a few blocks away. "Dad said he wouldn't be around (when the car was unearthed), 'but you boys will.' And we are."

Blissit, who now lives in Norman, Okla., and his brother, Richard, who still calls Tulsa home, are both involved in antique car ownership and restoration. Ron has restored three Pierce-Arrows, one of which, formerly owned by movie star Marlene Dietrich, was a winner at Pebble Beach. He still has a 1933 Pierce-Arrow and has a 1937 Packard in the wings as his next project.

Ron and Richard have offered to help the winner put the 50-year-old Plymouth into operating condition. "I still have all the special tools for those cars," said Blissit. "My dad thought I was crazy when I paid the Snap-On salesman $30 for a set of screwdrivers, but I still have them — with the lifetime warranty!" Ron went to Chrysler Master Mechanic school after high school graduation and became the youngest certified mechanic at age 18. After some years of oil field work, he operated a mechanic shop in Norman for many years.

"The question is," he says, "will we recognize the (Plymouth) when it comes out" of its courthouse square tomb. "If any moisture has gotten in, it's a dead duck." He plans to be on hand for the unveiling on June 15, and he's optimistic that the car will be in reasonable condition. What happens then?

"The worst thing," according to Blissit, "would be for someone to put in a battery and crank it over." Five gallons of gasoline were pumped into the tank before the burial. He says he'd pull the tank, clean it out along with the fuel system, put a kit in the fuel pump and rebuild the carburetor.

The brake master and wheel cylinders will need to be rebuilt. The engine, transmission and cooling system should be drained and refilled. Ron would pull the spark plugs and blow "pickling oil" into the cylinders, and lubricate everything.

Digging up a 50-year-old "new" Plymouth is shaping up as the most popular draw for the 2007 Oklahoma Centennial. A half-dozen car clubs are planning national meets in Tulsa, and at least two 1957 Plymouth Belvedere owners have said they will come for the event.

A Tulsarama Invitational Auto Show, limited to 125 cars, is scheduled for June 15-17 inside the Tulsa Convention Center. The 1957 Belvedere will be unveiled there at 6:30 p.m. Friday evening, after having been taken from the ground at noon. An open car show will occupy designated downtown parking lots close to the convention center on Saturday and Sunday.

Of course, everyone hopes the Plymouth will be in great condition — and worth 10 times the 1957 sticker price of approximately $2,800. If it falls short, the winner will still get a "trust fund" that started out at $100. Buried with the car and having accrued interest since 1957, it could be worth more than $500 by now.

A follow-up to this story is included on the next page.
CHAPTER 23: 1957 Plymouth Tulsarama! Aftermath, page 97

CHAPTER 23 | 1957 PLYMOUTH TULSARAMA! AFTERMATH
By Angelo Van Bogart & Matt Gergeni

SUNKEN TREASURE
Tulsarama! 1957 Plymouth found submerged in water

1957 Plymouth Belvedere at its display at the Tulsa Convention Center June 16. The car was unveiled the previous day.

A tattered and dirty cover and rusty exposed tailfin hinting at the buried 1957 Plymouth Belvedere's rusty condition didn't stop the sold-out crowd in the Maxwell Convention Center in Tulsa, Okla., from bursting into applause when the Plymouth's cover was pulled back from its nose.

Despite its condition, the weathered Plymouth, affectionately referred to as "Miss Belvedere" by Tulsarama! officials, remained the star of the Tulsarama! activities back on June 15, 2007. Once the car's cover was completely pulled back, it became obvious that the car had suffered from being completely submerged in its vault under the lawn of the Tulsa County Courthouse. It was also clear that the lowest two feet of the Plymouth had been submerged in water longer than the rest of the car, leaving an even line of darker corrosion around its bottom.

Making the car appear even worse were shredded remnants of the rust-colored and

The crowd gasped when the buried Belvedere was pulled from its resting place June 15.

white protective bag still clinging to areas of the skuzzy-looking, once-gold car's surface. (Think "Christine" at the start of the movie based on the Stephen King novel of the same name.)

The moisture also caused the car's rear springs to break, dropping the rear end of the car. It was rumored that pieces of the car's rear springs remained in the bottom of the vault, which was completely filled in with earth by the end of the day.

Rumors also spread that the nearby Tulsa County Courthouse suffered a water main break sometime in the mid-1970s, which may have been at least part of the cause for the tomb to show evidence of completely filling with water. When Tulsarama! officials checked on the tomb Wednesday before the car's unearthing, it was found to still contain several feet of water. Tulsarama! chairman Susan Davis Smith wasn't afraid to tell the crowd she was "devastated" upon learning the car's wet fate, but officials maintained the energy of the event throughout the weekend.

Several hours separated the car's rain-soaked unearthing from its vault at noon and its evening unveiling in the convention center, and hot rod-building celebrity Boyd Coddington and his crew used the time to determine if they might be able to start the car. Coddington's crew pulled back part of the car's rust-brown bag and opened the rusted hood during that time, but even the hot rodder conceded that the car should be left in its deteriorated condition, likely because he felt nothing could be done. Still, several of Boyd's employees began picking at sludge covering the trim and front bumper, exposing shiny areas and offering a

There's no starting this engine, which was just as crusty as the outside. Historians weren't sure which V-8 engine was in the Plymouth, but they learned it was a four-barrel engine once the hood was lifted.

false ray of hope.

Work immediately began by searching for the keys to the car and the container holding the microfilm with all of the 1957 entrants' guesses of the 2007 Tulsa population count. Since Boyd's workers couldn't open the doors, they forced the windows down (as 1957 photos show, the windows were left cracked open), and reached their arms into the decimated and slimy interior in search of keys, which couldn't be separated from the ignition. When the film canister was found in the backseat, it was found to have a gaping hole and no sign of the film.

Shockingly, most of the tires still held air, as well as the signatures of many of the people who signed the whitewalls before the car was dropped into the ground. Unfortunately, items placed into the trunk and passenger compartment didn't fare as well as the tires. Had many of the car's contents not been identified and remembered from 1957, the rusty and deformed Schlitz cans in the trunk and other artifacts may have never been positively identified. A cane and two glass jugs still containing gasoline were also removed from the Plymouth's trunk. The deck lid separated into two pieces upon opening.

While Coddington's crew buzzed around the Plymouth, the Tulsarama! committee members moved on to opening the keg-sized time capsule believed to contain an American

Left, Boyd Coddington's crew removed some of the scum covering the car to reveal a shiny bumper beneath. The sheet metal didn't fare as well.

Below, workers attempt to enter the Plymouth after its cover was removed. The doors were seized shut, and one of the windows was broken during the process, but they were finally able to lower both door windows.

flag and other items. Though this propane container-shaped item was as rusty looking as the larger Plymouth, it proved to be an excellent preserver of Tulsa history.

Once cracked open, the inside of the time capsule lid revealed a brilliant blue bumper sticker for the 1957 Tulsarama! event, as well as the American flag, notes from Tulsans and photos from the city in 1957, newspaper clippings and several other historic items. Most importantly, it also held the original entry blanks with population guesses, as well as the printed documents listing each contestant's name and 2007 population guess. Yes, someone will be identified as the new owner of the 1957 Plymouth with not only the lowest mileage, but also in the worst condition.

Officials also noted that the winner will receive the Plymouth and a 50-year-old savings certificate, but not the contents of the time capsule, which will go to the Tulsa Historical Society.

The Plymouth was displayed within the invitation-only car show at the Maxwell Convention Center in Tulsa. There, Tulsans and the city's thousands of visitors more closely examined the quarter-sized rust hole in the Plymouth's door, its completely decimated interior and bubbling metal.

Visitors agreed that, due to the car's poor condition, it should remain untouched as a keepsake of the optimism gifted by 1957 Tulsans looking to the future.

CHAPTER 24 — 1957 PONTIAC
By Phil Hall

A SOFT YEAR FOR A SHARP CAR
Pontiac sales dipped in 1957

Revised lines of the 1957 Pontiacs, which were on their third year of a styling cycle, can be seen on this Star Chief Custom Catalina four-door hardtop.

Looking at hard production numbers, the 1957 Pontiac was not a success. The tally of 334,041 was less than the 1956 run of 405,730 chiefs and way short of the 1955 record of 554,090 vehicles. Its new advertising tag of "America's Number 1 Road Car" didn't seem to help.

For the 1957 model run, Pontiac was in its third and final year of its styling cycle, as was sister General Motors division Chevrolet. Even though front and rear clips were altered from 1956 and earlier 1955 forms, Pontiac had to compete with radically all-new, lower-medium-priced cars from Chrysler Corp.'s Dodge and Ford Motor Co.'s Mercury. Even De Soto dipped down a notch to join in with its new Firesweep series.

Chrysler products featured "Forward Look" styling with large fins and a break from the past. Taking a similar departure was the 1957 Mercury with "Dream Car Design." Mercury also received its own body that season, breaking its lockstep with Fords of 1952-'56.

Like Chevrolet, which suffered sales problems with its face-lifted 1957 models, but went on to become an icon in later years,

101

The star of the 1957 Pontiac lineup was the mid-year, limited-production Star Chief Bonneville convertible. It featured a fuel injected V-8 and upgraded trim inside and out. It would become the highest collector-valued 1957 Pontiac for decades after its introduction.

1957 Pontiacs didn't attract all the customers expected when they were new. Pontiacs did, however, provide the collector market down the road with great-performing and good-handling cars, one of which is in the running for the highest-valued Pontiac of all times.

Part of the value of 1957 Pontiacs is historical. Once the choice of all too many old folks seeking comfort, Pontiac was transformed into a performance vehicle with the all-new 1955 models, which featured a new overhead-valve V-8 that had plenty of room to grow.

The engine started at 287.2 cubic inches in 1955, rose to 316.6 for 1956 and stopped at 347 for 1957. The 1957 engine displacement was only a stepping stone, as it would eventually follow the path to 389, 400, 421, 428 and 455 cubes.

However, the engine was only part of the story. On July 1, 1956, Semon "Bunkie" Knudsen took over as general manager of Pontiac Motor Division. At 43 years old, he had a vision of Pontiac being an exciting car that featured performance, and was raced in stock car and other events. Pontiac was never the same again.

The Star Chief Custom Safari four-door station wagon, billed as the "Transcontinental," was added to the 1957 Pontiac lineup mid-year. It featured revised exterior trim, chrome luggage rack and reclining lounge seating for the front passenger.

Though the 1957 design was already set when Knudsen took the helm, he was able to remove the Pontiac signature silver streaks that graced the hoods and trunks since 1935. That was not the only change.

He began a complicated system of engine options that included triple two-barrel carburetors, or "Tri-Power," as the setup was dubbed. Horsepower ramped up to 317 units in the version used in stock car racing. He made sure racing teams that wanted Pontiacs received them, with lightweight two-door sedans most often being used.

(Editor's note: see '57 Heaven article on page 34.)

When the Automobile Manufacturers Association banned factory racing and performance promotion in June of 1957, the other brands pulled in their horns. Pontiac did not. Knudsen openly defied the ban, and Pontiacs were raced, successfully, in 1958, 1959 and beyond.

The revised 1957 Pontiacs featured a juggled model lineup with Chieftain replacing Chieftain 860, Super Chief taking place of the Chieftain 870 series and Star Chief at the top in two sub-series: Star Chief and Star Chief Custom. All body styles from 1956 were continued, including the highly collectible Star Chief Custom Safari, the Pontiac two-door station wagon counterpart to the Chevrolet Bel Air Nomad.

But that was only the beginning. In January of 1957, two mid-year models were offered: the Star Chief Custom Safari four-door wagon, or "Transcontinental," and the Star Chief Bonneville convertible.

Ordinarily, the Safari four-door would have been the big attraction. It featured special anodized trim outside, a chrome luggage rack and special interior with a reclining lounge seat for the front passenger.

However, the Bonneville, using the name of a 1954 General Motors Motorama dream car, was one of 1957's major attractions. Outside, it, too, featured revised Star Chief trim, anodized aluminum panels and a trick interior, but the story was under the hood. Feeding its V-8 was mechanical fuel injection, similar to that found on the 1957 Chevrolet. At the time, horsepower ratings for the setup were not released. (Editor's note: Current sources estimate Bonneville engines were worth 315 hp.)

Listing for $5,782, the Bonneville was well above the Star Chief ragtop at $3,105. Supply was limited, and not all dealers could get Bonnevilles. When the counting was done, 630 went out the door. The combination of rareness, pioneering performance and special trim has driven Bonneville prices on the collector market into the six-figure range. With today's muscle car price frenzy, claiming the first Bonneville as the most valuable of all Pontiacs is a week-to-week proposition.

The Bonneville name went on to a long life at Pontiac on a wide variety of machinery, but the first is still the most sought after.

Knudsen and his Pontiac magic continued into the one-year 1958 models, but a severe recession proved even a worse gauge of his success, with production dropping to 217,303. Things turned around with the Wide-Track 1959 models, which topped 1957's sales, but even greater things were to come.

CHAPTER 25 — FORD'S 1957-'59 FORD RETRACTABLE

By Angelo Del Monte

50-PLUS YEARS OF FLIPPING TOPS
Ford's remarkable retractable

The 1957 Skyliner was a mechanical wonder. In less than one minute, the car could transform itself from a snug two-door hardtop to an open-air convertible.

In the America of the 1950s, anything seemed possible. And for the Ford Motor Co., that was especially true. Ambitious projects like brand new V-8s, two-seater Thunderbirds, a whole new line of cars and a reinterpretation of the classic Continental all seemed possible to Henry Ford II and his "Whiz Kids" that were running the show.

The Continental Mark II would be introduced as a prestige automobile whose ownership was nearly on an invitational basis. And along with this upcoming luxury

Although the retractable hardtop mechanism that eventually appeared on Ford Skyliners was originally intended for the Continental Mark II, the luxurious car never received it. All Continental Mark II coupes were conventional two-door hardtops.

coupe, Ford's engineers wanted to showcase their expertise by offering a retractable-roof version as well.

A disappearing hardtop automobile had always been a designer's dream and had even been realized on American prototypes in the '30s and '40s and some European cars. But could a steel roof that can vanish into the luggage compartment be built into a mass-produced vehicle? To help answer that question, a young engineer, Ben Smith, was lured from GM to Ford and placed in charge of making this dream a reality.

There was a secretive Special Products Division (SPD) that was at work on the Mark II, and from 1953 to 1955, Ben and his group worked on making the roof disappear. They tried hydraulics and a roof split in half; they tried a front-and-rear-opening trunk lid and a retracting rear window and found these were all unworkable. But they developed a power actuating screw jack, smaller electric motors, flexible shaft drives, ratcheting screw locks, multi-connectors and the means to make it all work at the push of a button. At a top-level meeting on Jan. 7, 1955, the Continental retractable made its first official showing. The roof

For 1958, the Skyliner received quad headlamps, just as many other cars of the model year did. With its top up, a Skyliner can be identified by its low roof, large rear flanks and a separation seam near the front of the top.

raised and lowered to the delight of upper management. The concept was now ready for mass production development.

The Continental was a car whose base sales figure was set to be a then-astronomical price of $10,000. Although thoroughly tested, the retractable mechanism was at this time deemed too risky to be offered on an automobile whose main mission was to set new standards in luxury vehicles.

While the SPD was developing the car and then showed that a retractable hardtop could be built, the marketing department conducted surveys. They discovered potential Mark II buyers were willing to pay a $2,500 premium for a retractable hardtop, which at the time was more than a brand-new Ford.

Ford's discovery showed that this might be an option that had a larger appeal than one that was only available on a limited-production vehicle. Why sell 2,000 a year when you might be able to sell 20,000, even if it sold for less per unit?

In the '50s, the largest growing segment of automotive styles was the hardtop. With hot-selling coupes, and then the widespread introduction of four-door hardtops in 1956, some felt that hardtops might replace traditional pillared vehicles altogether. Buyers might be lured into showrooms by flashy convertibles, but usually left buying more "practical" daily drivers. That convertible look was the hardtop's appeal. But a true hardtop convertible would be the best of both worlds.

The SPD's project, as it turned out, was not a very well-kept secret throughout Ford; and the Mercury, Lincoln and Ford divisions were becoming interested in its potential. "Whiz Kid" Robert McNamara coveted, and later received, the top job at Ford. But while he was Ford Division head, he wanted every reason for buyers to purchase a Ford. And what better way than to show the world that the latest automotive advancement — one that might completely replace soft-top convertibles — was another "Ford first?"

So in February 1955, Smith and the crew were given their second monumental task. They now had to graft the retractable hardtop mechanism onto the already well-along 1957 Ford.

In some ways, the design of the proposed all-new, lower-and-wider Ford was better suited to a hide-away hardtop design then the Mark II was. But still, changes needed to be made. Of course, the top had to be different. It was shorter and lower than the one found on the standard Ford. It had a more vertical rear window, a blind sail panel and a "flipper." The flipper was the front section of the roof that folded to shorten the top when it was lowered. The rear deck lid and rear fenders were longer than the standard version. The retractable also had an exclusive frame, body mounts, rims, gas tank and back seat. Although they look the same, even the side trim pieces are not interchangeable. Assembling retractables required special care, so they were relegated to their own production lines.

Three prototypes were made for testing. The retractable's scheduled introduction was always set to take place after the regular '57 Ford models. Actual production started a few months behind schedule, so one pre-production prototype was pressed into service for promotions. Painted and re-painted for numerous advertising photographs, this prototype was sent to the New York Auto Show in December 1956 for the car's first public showing.

Production started in March 1957, and now all that was needed was a name. A list of more than 1,000 names was trimmed to 126 finalists. On March 11, 1957, an Executive Communication from McNamara finalized the model's name, which was borrowed from the transparent-top Fords of '54-'56. And so it was christened the Ford Skyliner — the world's only hide-away hardtop.

The retractable debuts

On April 18, 1957, Ford dealers across the country displayed in their show rooms the all-new Ford Skyliner. Combining the

The last year for the Skyliner was 1959. Unlike soft-top convertibles, Skyliners didn't require a boot to conceal the lowered top. Instead, a package shelf filled the area where the folded material of a normal convertible was stored, providing a clean style line.

practicality and security of a hardtop design with the fun of an open convertible, Ford introduced a new automobile and the first crossover vehicle.

Utilizing mechanisms and designs developed for the 1956 Continental Mark II, the first mass-produced, fully automatic retractable top was brought to the public as a 1957-'59 Ford. Viewed by Ford as an amazing engineering advancement, it was considered a great draw for buyers to visit their Ford dealers. Hope was high that this design might actually replace the soft-top convertible, and Ford would be known as the innovator.

Longer, lower and wider than its '56 predecessors, the 1957 Ford was an all-new Ford right from the start. Stylish for its day, this car would go on to out-sell Chevrolet for the 1957 model year. The top-of-the-line Ford was the new Fairlane 500 model, and two convertibles were offered — the Sunliner, which was a conventional soft-top auto, and the ground-breaking Skyliner.

With the pull of a dash-mounted switch, the trunk deck would automatically unlock and open in the opposite direction of conventional automobile deck lids. While in the upright position, a rear package tray was unfolded from the trunk lid. Then the top unlocked from the windshield header and rear sail panel mounts. Electrically operated screw jacks helped raise the top and carry it to the trunk. While retracting, the front portion of the roof, known as the flipper, folded to enable the top to fit into the truck cavity. Once the top was nestled in the trunk, the rear deck lid closed and locked. The whole operation took just under one minute and could be reversed when the same switch was pushed.

Although only available on an abbreviated model year, the Skyliner sold 20,766 units for 1957, a promising start. Almost four times as many Sunliners were sold, but at a base price of $2,942, the Skyliner was Ford's most costly family car offered that year.

For 1958, Ford offered a facelift on all models, including the Skyliner. This year's Fairlane 500 borrowed styling cues from the all-new four-passenger Thunderbird. One of the most notable differences on this new model was 1958's hottest styling trend — quad headlights. Another trend for the year was an economic downturn known as the Eisenhower recession. Across the board, automotive sales were down, and the Skyliner was no exception. Only 14,713 were produced for 1958.

A redesigned Ford was offered for 1959, and the Skyliner was part of the lineup. Since more time was available to work on this design, the retractable mechanism was improved and actually melded into the car more seamlessly. The flipper was made shorter, which, in turn, made for a shorter trunk cavity. All '59 Ford roofs now had a blind sail panel, so, overall, the Skyliner looked more like its stable mates than the previous years' models. Midway through the year, Ford introduced a new top-of-the-line series — the Galaxie. Both convertible models migrated to this upscale line. Most Ford models posted better sales than 1958, but the Skyliner only sold 12,915 units for the model year.

Even though sales declined for its three-year model run, and probably because design work started before these numbers were known, a 1960 retractable was planned. The retractable project had been done on a "contract" basis between the Continental and Ford divisions — the first and very likely only time this was done at the company. But by the time the 1960 models were being designed, the engineering team that designed the original mechanism had already been disbanded. The project was handed over to a group of engineers that five years earlier had told the Special Products Division that building a retractable was not possible. After six months and expenditures of several hundred thousand dollars, they proved themselves correct.

When in operation, the hide-away hardtop still turns heads 50-plus years after its debut. Skyliners continue to be popular with collectors, but never appreciated as much as one might think for a vehicle this unique. In fact, the Sunliner often commands higher dollars because fewer survive.

Now, after years of being relegated to the 1950s fad bin like a discarded hula hoop, the Skyliner seems to have developed its share of imitators. The retractable convertible concept has been reintroduced by both domestic and foreign automakers.

So now we are again free to ask: Is there a Ford retractable in our future?

CHAPTER 26 | 1958 BUICK
By Phil Hall

BUICK'S 'CHROME DOMES'
Gilded 1958s were the last in a line of '50s auto excess

Lots of chrome and aluminum trim and less popularity marked the 1958 Buick models. This Special Riviera two-door hardtop shows off its revised lines and new grille with 160 sparkling squares.

Critics like to point to the 1958 Buick as an example of domestic car excess in the 1950s. Indeed, it was a product dripping in excess, especially when it came to bright exterior trim. Its dated, heavy styling arrived just in time for a recession and fallout in new car sales.

Truth is, 1958 Buick was not alone in its plight in 1958. Oldsmobile suffered the same fate and, to a lesser extent, so did Mercury and Edsel.

While the 1958 Buicks seemed a logical transition from the 1957 models at the time of design, the planning all took place before the futuristic 1957 Chrysler Corp. products came out boasting low roof lines, big fins and airy greenhouses.

It wouldn't be until 1959 that General Motors was able to answer, with Buick being among the most radically changed.

New at the top of the Buick lineup for 1958 was the Limited series. It had slightly less bright trim and a longer stretch in the rear quarters. This Riviera four-door hardtop was Buick's entry in the near luxury field.

The model year wasn't a good one for business, no matter what the styling, with the only exceptions to the sales downturn being the compact Ramblers and totally re-done four-passenger Ford Thunderbirds.

Buick, however, apparently wasn't living in fear when the 1958s were introduced, touting "Air Born B-58 Buicks" that "Look and feel like flight on wheels." Literature and advertising featured the Convair B-58 Hustler delta-wing bomber, which was also not a roaring success.

Styling started up front with a die-cast grille comprised of 160 squares of chrome and flanked by directional signal/parking lamps. There were now dual (quad) headlights and a slightly raised hood with a big "V" emblem in the center and four horizontal chrome strips. Gone were the Ventiports (portholes) that were on the front fenders since the 1949 models. Also gone were the full rear-wheel cutouts, giving the cars a heavier look.

Side trim varied, depending on the series, but all except the top-line Limited received a large cove of bright trim on the rear third that drew most of the "excess" criticism.

The amount of bright trim varied from "too much" to "well beyond." A double-bar rear bumper had large pods on each end and a cove of more bright trim between the bars.

Thankfully, the wind splits that divided the rear windows into three pieces on some 1957 models were gone.

Power was unchanged from 1957 with the 364-cid V-8 the only engine. It was rated at 250 hp in most Special models (210 hp with standard shift) and, again, was good for 300 for the rest of the gang. However, it had a new name — again, going for excess — with the B-12000 tag. Literature said it "develops a thrust of 12,000 pounds behind every piston's power stroke." Somehow, this rating system never caught on.

Flight Pitch Dynaflow was standard on the Limited and Roadmaster 75, while the previous year's Variable Pitch Dynaflow came standard in the Super and Century and

Dual headlamps were a new feature for 1958 Buicks, giving the assembly line employees more to do to get them focused. Here at the factory in Flint, Mich., a worker uses a pair 22-inch lenses and photo-electric cells to get the heavily chromed new Buick on the beam.

optional on the Special.

The lineup for 1958 was revised from the final 1957 tally. Special Series 40 models on a 122-inch wheelbase had seven models again: two- and four-door sedans, two- and four-door Riviera hardtops, a convertible and two wagons, the pillared Estate Wagon and hardtop Riviera Estate Wagon. The Century Series 60, also on a 122-inch stretch, had five choices with no two-door sedan or pillared wagon like the Specials had. Its hardtop wagon was called "Caballero."

The Super Series 50, on a 127 1/2-inch wheelbase, was simpler, with just two- and four-door Riviera hardtops.

Gone was the plain Roadmaster. The next step up was the Roadmaster Series 75 — a series introduced mid-year in 1957. On a 127 1/2-inch wheelbase, it had three models, adding a convertible to the Super's pair of styles.

New for 1958 was the Limited Series 700. It was the first use of the Limited name since the 1942 models and turned out to be a one-year wonder. It shared the Super and Roadmaster 75 wheelbase and model lineup. At 227.1 inches long, it came in eight inches longer than the 75 and Super and more than 15 inches beyond the smaller cars.

Like other manufacturers, Buick offered optional air suspension in the 1958 models and, like other manufacturers, Buick's system was not a success.

Not everything Buick did for 1958 could

THE BUICK "WELLS FARGO"
Built Especially for Dale Robertson

The Buick "Wells Fargo" convertible built for TV star Dale Robertson made the auto show rounds for 1958. The Limited convertible featured wood side trim, special interior features and appeared with the star of "Tales of Wells Fargo" on a postcard handed out at the shows.

be termed excessive. A display model dubbed the "Wells Fargo" was utilized on the auto show circuit. It was a Limited convertible said to be made especially for TV star Dale Robertson. The car featured a tasteful wood inlay in place of the chrome cove on the sides. The husky-voiced Robertson starred in the Buick-sponsored NBC-TV program "Tales of Wells Fargo" in the western era on prime-time television. The show car featured leather-trimmed bucket seats, a rifle rack, gun holsters on the doors and cowhide carpeting.

Buick set a production record of 738,814 units for the 1955 model year. The company held down third place in sales. That number dropped to 572,024 for 1956 and 405,086 for the 1957 models when Plymouth booted Buick down to fourth. Things became worse for the 1958 models with 241,892 built and the also-over-chromed Oldsmobile taking fourth ranking.

The 1959 Buicks were really all-new. Not only were the finned new offerings completely restyled, but all the old series names were dropped (at least for a while). New designations, such as LeSabre, Invicta and Electra, booted out Special, Century, Super, Roadmaster and Limited.

While the domestic new-car market picked up some for 1959, Buick sales did not. Traditional buyers — of which Buick had many — were left cold, and only 232,579 finned machines were built.

Buick was in deep trouble. The overdone 1958 models may have been part of the problem, but there was much more that needed fixing.

CHAPTER 27 | **1958-'60 EDSEL**

By Bill Siuru

WHAT'S RARER THAN AN EDSEL?

An Edsel convertible, of course

Ford touted the Edsel as "The Newest Thing on Wheels" and as a car that would be "recognizable a block away." The 1958 Edsel, with its sculptured fenders, horse-collar grille and gobs of chrome, accomplished that.

But while Ford set a sales goal of 100,000 units annually, only 110,847 Edsels total were built in its three model years. And of these, only 4,225 were ragtops.

For its initial year, Edsel offered two distinct model ranges. At the lower end there were the Ranger and Pacer that shared much with the Ford, including their 118-inch wheelbases. At the other end there were the Mercury-based Corsair and Citation on Mercury's 124-inch wheelbase. Pacer and Citation both had convertible options — 1,876 Pacer and 930 Citation convertibles were built.

When Ford realized the Edsel was not selling well, the company cut back on the number of models and offered only the Ford-based Edsels, now designated the Ranger and Corsair (the more deluxe Corsair replaced the Pacer). Only Corsair offered a convertible, and 1,343 were built.

For the very abbreviated 1960 model

Prototypes for the Edsel included a convertible.

year (just more than a month), only 2,846 Rangers and Villager station wagons were built, including just 76 convertibles.

Mechanically, the 1958 Edsels had several industry firsts, including self-adjusting brakes, a transmission that locked in park

A 1959 Edsel Corsair convertible.

The optional continental kit made this 1958 Pacer look even longer.

until the ignition key turned, electrically controlled interior release for the front-hinged hood and 60/40 split front seats. In 1958, two V-8 engines were offered: a 361-cid, 303-hp mill in the Ford-based Edsels and 410-cid, 345-hp engine in the bigger Edsels.

Another innovation was Edsel's Teletouch automatic transmission. While Mercury, Packard and Chrysler all offered pushbutton controls, the Edsel's transmission was the most radical since it was located in the center of the steering wheel. Planetary gears in the steering column kept the buttons stationary while the steering wheel was turned.

Besides dropping models for 1959, the styling was much more subdued. The 410-cid V-8 was dropped, as was Teletouch transmission. Corsair convertibles featured

Then Vice President Richard Nixon rides in a 1958 Edsel during a visit to Lima, Peru. Could there be a more fitting vehicle for the future failed President?

Even though ragtops accounted for a fraction of total Edsel sales, they were featured in Edsel advertising.

a 332-cid V-8, with the 361-cid V-8 as optional.

The 1960 Edsels were really just rebadged Fords. The upstanding grille gave way to a horizontal one that fit into the same space as the Ford's grille. Only the rear sheet metal, including the upstanding four tail lamps, was unique to the Edsel. Indeed, it is relatively easy to graft unique 1960 Edsel sheet metal onto a 1960 Ford Sunliner to create a much rarer, and more valuable, 1960 Ranger convertible. Since counterfeits are around, if you are considering a 1960 Edsel ragtop, look carefully to make sure all the numbers match.

CHAPTER 28 | **1958 FARGO TRUCKS**

By James Mays

CANADIAN TWIST
Fargo trucks filled Chrysler Corp.'s truck void

For the Canadian market, Dodge trucks were badged as "Fargos." This step side hails from 1958. (James Mays collection)

Long respected by Canadians in the truck field, Fargo had been sold throughout the Dominion of Canada by Chrysler-Plymouth dealers beginning in 1936. Model for model, the badge-engineered Fargo was designed to match its Dodge counterparts, but was sold at Canadian Chrysler-Plymouth dealerships throughout the 10 provinces. Like Dodge, Fargo enjoyed a solid reputation for generous capacity and rugged construction. Under the watchful eye of corporate stylist Virgil Exner, Chrysler's truck lines benefitted from the new "Forward Look" in 1957, and could brag of sleek styling.

For the 1958 selling season, Exner's magic touch for the Fargo pickup trucks extended to the latest industry rage — quad headlights. The face of the 1958 Fargo

Power-Master was rugged and bold. Fargo was blessed with a slim, modern grille, a graceful application of Exner's famed "forward thrust" to the down-sloping hood and overall crisp, clean lines finished in single solid colors or optional tasteful two-tone color combinations.

Designated as being part of the D Series, the 1958 Fargo Power-Master trucks were advertised as "Built to fit your Job!" and "New and ready to work for you." Lest good looks not tell the story on its own, styling was hammered home to the salesmen as an important selling point. Advertising bragged shamelessly that Fargo was "a leader for looks as well as function." To drive the point home even further, salesmen were trained to point out to prospective customers that the Fargo's new looks promoted new safety.

"Driver-relaxing Fargo cab is safety itself!" shrilled the advertising. The Full-View wrap-around windshield offered an enormous 1,023 square inches of vision area "to let you see more of the road ahead." A moderate extra-cost option appeared in the form of a wrap-around rear window, offering Wide-Scope view at the rear of the cab. All Fargo pickups boasted an alligator-type hood that opened to a full 90-degree angle for complete engine access, as well as to a less-gaping 45-degree angle for routine maintenance.

Inside the stylish haulers, cabs were trimmed in a new Sandalwood color that "retains its good looks through months of hardest service." The new Safety-Centre steering wheel was 18 inches in diameter (20 inches on the Fargo D700 models). The size was calculated by engineers to give an exact and true grip needed for safe steering. The new design reduced the probability of injury in the event of an accident.

The D100 models included an express pickup on a 108-inch wheelbase, fitted with a 6-1/2-foot box or a 116-inch wheelbase with a 7-1/2-foot-box. A panel truck was also offered. Maximum capacity was 5,000 pounds. The 1958 Fargo D100 Express, with the 6-1/2-foot box installed, sold for $2,555. The D100 Panel carried a list price of $2,595.

The standard engine for the D100 was the rugged L-head six, "proved in billions of miles of use." It was mated to the exceptionally quiet steering column-mounted, three-speed manual transmission. As optional equipment, a 184-hp, dome-shaped combustion chamber V-8 engine was available as was the four-speed manual or the fancy, space-age pushbutton LoadFlite Automatic Drive.

The Fargo D300 was offered with the L-head mill and the special four-speed Synchro-Silent transmission as standard equipment. These models rode on a 126-inch wheelbase, permitting installation of a king-sized 9-foot bed. The D300 models were rated at a 9,000-lb. maximum gross vehicle weight and could be ordered in a wide choice of standard or special bodies, depending on the customer's requirements. The 314-cid V-8 was optional. With a list price of $2,570 for the 1958 Fargo D300, on its generous 126-inch wheelbase, the truck was a natural choice for farm operations.

For real workhorse duty, there was the Fargo Model D400 in the 10,000- to 15,000-lb. GVW range. These big Fargos rode on a 129-inch or a 153-inch wheelbase. In addition to the rugged deep-frame construction, the 400s boasted dual rear wheels. The L-head six-cylinder engine was standard equipment and mated to the four-speed manual on the D400 models, but the 192-hp V-8 was available as an extra-cost item as was the heavy-duty five-speed synchronized transmission. "Steering is light and easy, [the] cab's a real pace-setter for comfort." Fargo's D400 chassis and cab models ranged in price from $2,934* to $2,965.

Further up the scale, the D500 could handle tough jobs with plenty of muscle to spare in the 19,500- to 34,000-GVW class. Wheelbase choices were 141, 153 or 171 inches and were created to take plenty of punishment. The 153-inch-wheelbase chassis and cab for the 1958 Fargo D500 sold for $3,417 and weighed in at 5,060 lbs. If that wasn't enough to get the customer to sign, the salesman was instructed to say, "And for all its stamina, the Fargo D500 is the handsomest truck in its weight class."

Last but not least, Fargo fielded the D700, the first time it entered the 25,000- to 50,000-lb. class. Wheelbases were listed at 129, 141, 153 or 171 inches. These mammoth workhorses were all fitted with the Chrysler-engineered 218-hp, hemispheric combustion V-8, to "give you the power you need to take any job in stride." The brawny Fargo's mill was coupled to a five-speed manual transmission. When riding the 171-inch wheelbase, the 1958 Fargo D700 chassis and cab listed for $3,483.

As a truck offering conceived to generate brand loyalty for Chrysler-Plymouth dealers, the Fargo was never as popular as its Dodge kin. Fargo model-year production for 1953 amounted to 6,134 units. In 1954, that number slipped downward to 5,317 units. In 1955, the number dropped again as only 3,454 Fargo trucks had been built. The total for 1956 was encouraging, as 4,750 units were built, and the 1957 total rose again ever so slightly to reach 4,816 units. A recession hit the country, and calendar-year production for 1958 was off by a wide margin, as only 3,018 Fargo trucks were assembled in Chrysler Canada's Windsor, Ontario, plant.

Editor's Note:
Prices are listed in Canadian dollars.

CHAPTER 29 | **1958 STUDEBAKER HAWK**

By Bill McCleery

HEAVENLY HAWK
'58 Studebaker remains a 'Golden' oldie

Ed Reynolds, of Greenfield, Ind., finally got his hands on his dream car a year ago when he bought an original 1958 Studebaker Golden Hawk.

Passion for Studebakers runs in Ed Reynolds' blood. His father was an engineer at the automaker's South Bend, Ind., headquarters until the company discontinued production at its Indiana plant in 1964.

Nowadays, the younger Reynolds runs a worldwide Studebaker parts business from his Greenfield, Ind., home. He also is president of the Studebaker Drivers Club. Once in a while, he'll buy an old Studebaker — though at this stage, he says, it generally requires a special car to come along before he gets interested in buying.

That happened a couple summers ago when Reynolds acquired a 1958 Golden Hawk he had first seen more than 30 years ago, when he was a schoolteacher near Pomona, Calif. Any '58 Golden Hawk is a relatively rare car. Studebaker produced only 878 such cars that year, according to figures from the Studebaker Drivers Club.

During its three years of production, the Golden Hawk was literally one of the fastest cars on the road. In its inaugural year of 1956, the Golden Hawk was powered by a 352-cubic-inch Packard en-

The fins on the '58 Golden Hawk were certainly a sign of the times, but didn't seem overdone.

gine with 275 hp. In 1957 and 1958, the Golden Hawk came with a 289-cubic-inch Studebaker engine — but with a centrifugal supercharger that made the small V-8's performance on par with much larger engines.

Advertisements in 1958 touted the Golden Hawk as "America's first family-size sports car."

The '58 specimen purchased by Reynolds was as rough around the edges. After Reynolds got the car home to Indiana, he found about 20 dead mice burrowed into various crevices of the car. And at some point in the life of the car, a bag of dry dog food apparently spilled.

"I found pieces of dog food everywhere," Reynolds said.

The combination of dead mice, dog food and other possible contaminants left their mark. "It still smells in there even though I've cleaned it out," Reynolds said.

But the car is a solid, all-original survivor, right down to its faded gold paint. Despite the fact it had sat in a garage for much of the past decade without being started or driven, the car's 289-cubic-inch engine performs just fine since a rebuild of its supercharger and carburetor. Reynolds also replaced the fuel pump and a badly dented gas tank.

Reynolds likes the fact his car is almost identical to a prototype 1958 Golden Hawk assigned to his father by Studebaker Corp. as a company car. "He probably had it nine months," Reynolds recalled.

Since purchasing the Golden Hawk, Reynolds has wavered on his plans for the car.

"I bought it thinking I'd restore it," he said. "It's so nice and original, though, I almost hate to mess with it. And if you were going to restore it, it would need everything in order to be done right. It doesn't just need a paint job. You'd need new chrome, new interior. You'd want to go ahead and rebuild the engine while you had it out for detailing. It would be endless."

Reynolds is thinking he might just enjoy the car as-is for a few years. He likes the car for its clean lines and smooth design. Its fins, for example, are tasteful — not gaudy or overdone.

"Sometimes I'll just see it sitting in the garage and just look at it," Reynolds said. "It's a very pretty car."

On Friday nights, Reynolds sometimes drives the car to a cruise-in held weekly in the parking lot of a shopping mall on the Eastside of Indianapolis. People seem drawn to the car amid the more common Fords, Chevys and Mopars. It's something different from the usual 1960s muscle cars and shiny street rods.

"I almost always get comments," Reynolds said. "Several people have told me it was their favorite car there."

The car is equipped with dual radio antennas sprouting from its back fins and power windows. It lacks power seats, an option sold on some Golden Hawks.

Two other models of cars in 1958 were sisters to the Golden Hawk — the Packard Hawk and the Studebaker Silver Hawk. The Silver Hawk was a step beneath the Golden Hawk while the Packard version of the car was in many respects a top-of-the-line model in its own right.

The Studebaker-Packard Corp. — the company's name after Studebaker's 1954 marriage with Packard — produced even fewer Packard Hawks in 1958 than Studebaker Golden Hawks. A total of 588 Packard Hawks came off the assembly line that year, according to Studebaker Drivers Club information. The 1958 model year was the end of the line for the Packard name.

Reynolds remains open to the idea of someday restoring the Golden Hawk. Meanwhile, he has other projects to keep him busy. Besides operating his business — Studebaker International Inc. (www.studebaker-intl.com) — he's finishing the restoration of a 1960 Studebaker Lark – a two-door sedan — and he's trying to solve a few problems besetting his restored 1928 Studebaker Dictator Roadster.

"For more information about the Studebaker Drivers Club, log onto: www.studebakerdriversclub.com

CHAPTER 30 | **1959 CADILLAC FLEETWOOD SIXTY SPECIAL**

Story and photos by Bill Rothermel

50 YEARS LATER... STILL SPECIAL

Few cars will ever match the glitz and glamour of the '59 Fleetwood Sixty Special

Cadillac produced 12,550 Fleetwood Sixty Specials for 1959. Dave and Dora Forry of Manheim, Pa., own this one.

It seems almost impossible that more than 60 years have passed since the first tailfin graced the hindquarters of the then-new 1948 Cadillac. Thanks to a General Motors stylist named Harley Earl, fins would become a Cadillac trademark through 1964. Earl gained his inspiration from World War II Lockheed P-38 Lightning aircraft whose rear wing the Cadillac would mimic.

124

As the '50s evolved, so did the tailfin. They became progressively larger with each passing year, but not until the arrival of Virgil Exner at Chrysler Corp. did things take on proportions of a grand magnitude. While Earl is credited for first using the tailfin as a design element, it was Exner who took things to extremes. Exner penned Chrysler's now legendary "Suddenly it's '60" styling for 1957, sending competitors back to the drawing boards. Quite literally overnight, Chrysler became Detroit's styling leader, causing everyone else to play catch-up.

General Motors, it is said, abandoned the designs its stylists were working on and sought immediately to gain styling superiority. If the 1958 Buick Limited is recognized as the hallmark of excessive chrome, the 1959 Cadillac, designed by Dave Holls, was the undisputed king of fins. According to the late Holls, the massive fins were the result of a directive from top management at Cadillac that the company was not to be outdone — by anyone! No single automotive design better symbolizes the flamboyant '50s than the 1959 Cadillac.

The Sixty Special name made its first appearance as part of Cadillac's 1938 model lineup. It was a derivative of the Series 60, the division's least expensive line of cars (moving upmarket in later years). The Bill Mitchell-designed four-door sedan was a styling masterpiece employing a new X-chassis that enabled the body to rest within the frame while providing the stiffest chassis on the market. In combination with a wheelbase three inches longer than the standard 60 Series cars, the Sixty Special was also three inches lower than its siblings. Running boards were omitted, as was the typical beltline trim, giving the car a sleek appearance that made it appear even lower still. The Sixty Special remained a part of the Cadillac lineup through 1972 (eventually returning in 1987).

The Sixty Special always signified something unique and, well, special in the Cadillac lineup. That held true for 1959 as well. The Sixty Special was a sedan until 1957, when it adopted the hardtop sedan styling of the rest of the Cadillac line. However, it retained its own distinctive moldings and trim. For 1959, the unique Sixty Special trim included side-mounted dummy air scoops on the rear fenders along with a thin chrome bead from the front fender back to the rear bumper and then forward once again to the front wheel well. The fin-mounted tail lamps were chromed, not body color, as they were on lesser models. Cadillac produced 12,550 for the 1959 model year. Dave and Dora Forry of Manheim, Pa., are the lucky owners of one of those rare '59 Sixty Specials.

The Forrys' car sat for sale along Route 462 in south-central Pennsylvania for months. Dave heard about the car, but had no interest in a four-door. Three months later, Dora passed by the Caddy and noticed that it wasn't just an ordinary Cadillac sedan. After realizing it was a Sixty Special (with air suspension, no less), the couple checked out the car and found it was rust-free and had an odometer reading of just 15,000 miles! Needless to say, they quickly made arrangements to purchase the car and arrange for delivery.

While Dora was signing the papers, Dave was doing necessary repairs — in the parking lot — to make the car road worthy for the trip home. When Dave turned the key, the engine turned right over. Much to his surprise, the air suspension also worked just fine. "The car felt great," he said.

What followed was a four-year restoration completed in August 2008. While Dave was working on the car, an owner's card was found inside with a Cumberland, Md., address on it. "Capitol Cadillac," the famous Washington, D.C. Cadillac dealer, was inscribed in pencil on top of the radio, leading the couple to believe that the car might have been originally sold there.

While the body was never removed from the frame, a comprehensive restoration included all chrome, glass, interior, carpet and paint, with Dave doing all but the upholstery and a portion of the paintwork himself. The door panels are original, but the leather was dried out and cracked, necessitating replacement. The Ebony Black exterior perfectly complements the interior, a combination of white leather and black Colony cloth.

In addition to the air-suspension, a $215 option when new, the car is loaded with extras, including power vent windows, power door locks, power trunk release and pull-down, Autronic Eye, cruise control, fog lamps, signal-seeking radio with floor foot switch and air conditioning, which was $474 in 1959!

The expert restoration received its Senior badge and a first-place at the Cadillac-LaSalle Club Grand National meet in Cherry Hill, N.J., at its first showing, which came within hours after its restoration was complete. In addition, the car was given its AACA First Junior at Hershey, Pa., as well as the Best Restoration and Detailing Award at the Lancaster, Pa., Artistry in Motion Vintage Grand Tour and Show.

The Forrys are a Cadillac family — they also own an award-winning 1964 deVille convertible and are restoring a '59 Eldorado Biarritz. It too, has air suspension. "It's like restoring three cars, it's so complicated," Dave joked.

While he was standing back and admiring his Fleetwood the first time he saw it more than five years ago, Dave says a group of teenagers drove by, slowed down and yelled out, "That's the ugliest car we've ever seen."

They probably wouldn't say that now.

CHAPTER 31 | *1959 De SOTO AT DAYTONA*

By Angelo Van Bogart

DAYTONA DESTINY

A 1959 De Soto's adventure from assembly line to starting line

Bernie Hentges' 1959 De Soto Firedome, car No. 81, at speed while qualifying for the 1959 Daytona 500. The Minnesotan qualified 12th and earned 37th place after driving his race car to the race.

When most people buy a new car off a dealer's lot, they use it to fetch groceries, drive to work and carry their family to church. Not Bernie Hentges. When the 22-year-old bought a gleaming new 1959 De Soto, it was with one thing in mind — racing at the newly built Daytona International Speedway.

Racing on the new track, which had replaced the sandy beaches used at Daytona until the new track opened in 1959, wasn't an honor earned overnight. Hentges had built a strong reputation racing MoPars around his Johnsonville, Minn., home through the 1950s. He had done so well, he caught the attention of Chrysler Corp. officials who even gave him parts and sometimes cars to drive.

"[Chrysler Corp.] had scouts, and if you had a few real good seasons, you would be recognized [with a factory-backed car].

"Wayzata Motors sold me a car ... a D-500," Hentges said. "About mid-year, they came out with the D-500-1. I don't know if it's true, but I was told they were only given for racing. I was able to buy it and they gave me all the racing parts for it.

"[The D-500-1] had the Imperial suspension and brakes and was based on the Coronet, the least-expensive model they could put the parts on that there was in 1956."

While the car was fast enough to main-

The De Soto in the garage area of the Daytona International Speedway during the week of the 1959 Daytona Race.

tain Hentges' growing legend status on Minnesota dirt tracks, it posed several mechanical challenges.

"Every race I was in, I lost an engine," he said. "I went through eight engines in eleven races."

From working in his father-in-law's garage, Hentges was as good under the hood as he was behind the wheel, and it didn't take him long to determine the source of his engine troubles — motor oil that wasn't up to the rigors Hentges put it through.

"Every time the engine oil temperature would reach 260 degrees [it would blow]," Hentges said. "Late in the season, I went back to the oil I was using before, Phillips 66 Trop-Arctic, and didn't blow anymore engines with that oil."

About this time, Chrysler's Bert Carter was watching the races at the Minnesota State Fairgrounds and caught Hentges racing one of his company's cars, the 1956 Dodge D-500-1. Hentges led the race the first 20-30 laps when the predictable happened — the engine blew. Luckily, Hentges was figuring out the source of his engine problems when Carter invited him to Detroit in 1957 to discuss racing MoPars. Hentges arrived with some suggestions.

"I went to Detroit and waited in the office a good three hours before I went to talk to him," Hentges said. "I told them, 'the problem I am seeing is you are having lubrication problems.'" Carter told Hentges that the Automotive Manufacturers Association (AMA) had agreed not to sponsor race cars, and that he did not have good enough parts for racing at the time. (However, according to Hentges, General Motors and Ford continued to sponsor race cars.) Hentges left without a sponsor after Carter told him, "We don't have anything good enough to race for you."

The 1956 D-500-1 Dodge followed Hentges from Minnesota to his first NASCAR race at Daytona in 1957 where his mechanical luck didn't get any better.

"It was a two-lane road and I couldn't pass," Hentges said of the sandy Daytona track. "If somebody got behind you, they would push. At that time, the cars weren't as nearly closely matched as they are today, but back then, it was a several-second difference between the cars. I got behind another guy and was pushing him, and then I got pushed. My hood buckled and I was looking through a slot four inches (between the lifted hood and the cowl), and your whole depth of field changes. As we came up the corner, I thought I was closer than we were, but I was going about 110 miles per hour and downshifted and the transmission blew up. It was my own fault."

In 1958, Hentges kept his racing closer to home and stuck with MoPar products. He acquired a 1958 Plymouth with a 350-cid V-8 and two four-barrel carburetors, but when Hentges raced on the IMCA circuit, he had to install a single carburetor. The Plymouth also received some Imperial suspension components from the D-500-1 Dodge.

"I had pretty good success with it, and if I didn't wreck it, I finished in the top cars."

The following year, Hentges received an invitation to run in the Daytona 500 on the new Daytona International Speedway. The honor to drive on the new track was too good to pass up, and even though he was lacking in funds, he bought himself a car and made plans to attend the race.

"When I got the invitation to Daytona in 1959, I knew I wanted a Plymouth or a Dodge with the 383 engine, but there were none available in the five-state area," Hentges said. He found a beige De Soto Firedome two-door hardtop, which came standard with a 383-cid engine off the showroom floor, but he only had two to three weeks to get it ready and make it to the race. Hentges didn't fear the deadline, or the repercussions his lack of financing might cause.

"I drove it 14 miles to my [future] father-in-law's garage, took the upholstery out, the [D-500-1] hubs and spindles off the Plymouth and put them on the De Soto."

Hentges also removed the front clip to make it easier to access the suspension system and to beef up the chassis.

"There was a box frame on [those De Sotos], and they were only spot welded, so I welded the frame solid," Hentges said. "I put gussets on all of the corners of the cross member, on the front frame where the stabilizer went across. I changed the A arms and the rest of the Imperial suspension, [and took] off the wheels from my Plymouth and put them on the De Soto."

The De Soto's automatic transmission was also removed in favor of the Plymouth manual transmission, and the car was fitted with manual steering. To get all the gauges he needed in one convenient pod, Hentges installed the Plymouth's instrument cluster on the transmission hump of the De Soto's floor.

The 383-cid De Soto wedge-head engine received an Isky cam, solid lifters, new push rods and miked head gaskets under CC-ed heads.

Driving the De Soto to Daytona

While the weather in Daytona is nice in February, that's rarely the case in Minnesota. Hentges expected to tow his De Soto to the Florida race behind a truck, but a snowstorm made the roads slick and Hentges found it impossible to keep the truck and car on the road. After investing so much time and energy into preparing the De Soto for the first race at Daytona International Speedway, Hentges wasn't about to let some flakes get in his way. He re-installed the headlamps and taillamps into the De Soto and drove the car south with his girlfriend (and future wife) Rita sharing part of the front seat. (That front seat had been pulled from Hentges' previous Plymouth race car and installed in the De Soto for the race.) Even more shocking to anyone who's ever driven in a Midwest snow storm, Hentges made the trip on a set of Firestone Super Sports race tires!

"We drove the De Soto down there on the racing tires, which are a real hard compound," Hentges said, adding the car still had its radio, heater and all the glass to make the long drive somewhat comfortable. To carry the extra parts that would not fit in the De Soto's trunk, such as an extra pair of tires, the truck was driven behind Hentges' De Soto.

Before Hentges even left, many of racing's legends were already at the new track, competing their qualifying runs and tweaking their cars to the new track. On his drive down, Hentges tuned in his radio to hear the reports coming from the track and caught Fireball Roberts' qualifying time through the De Soto's speaker. Hentges began to get nervous by the numbers he was hearing.

"I didn't think I would be able to beat Fireball Roberts," he said. During the drive to Daytona, Hentges determined a way using his tachometer to figure out if he would be able to get in the 130-mph range the other drivers were running in.

"We got on a highway at one or two in the morning, and I told the drivers [of the truck] to go ahead one mile, and if there isn't anybody ahead, blink your headlights."

After the truck traveled ahead one mile and blinked its headlamps, Hentges flogged the De Soto up to speed.

"I calculated how fast I would be going by the rpms in that mile and [determined] I went 135 mph ... I figured I might be able to make it." When he did make it to the track, Hentges' qualifying speed was 134 mph.

"That car went pretty doggone good."

Wide open in a De Soto

Upon emerging from a tunnel onto the track, Hentges was in awe. "The track is enormous, and I had never driven on asphalt," he said.

Time was running short, so almost immediately, Hentges was instructed to get his physical. Just then, he ran into a couple of racing buddies from Minnesota who didn't have a car or a way onto the track, so they volunteered to join Hentges' small pit crew.

"We got in and the first thing they did was pre-race inspection before you got on the track," he said. "They had to make sure everything you did was to their standards. We did remove one cylinder head to make sure they weren't milled, and we had to pull out one axle to make sure we didn't have it locked."

Then the officials noticed something wrong — the De Soto had tall and skinny tires with deep treads for dirt track racing, not the wider tires appropriate for asphalt.

After a race official waved over the Firestone representative who was on hand, Hentges was able to work out a deal for the right tires that didn't obliterate his shoestring budget.

"[The Firestone representative] told me the tires were $80 apiece, but was willing to trade for my dirt track tires. He asked me how many miles I had on the tires and said, 'I'll trade you.'"

But the rush was on for Hentges to qualify the De Soto for the race, and there was no time for new tires.

"I had just gotten there — everybody else had been there two weeks — and they waved me up to qualify. So I just went ahead on the track."

And qualify he did. Hentges and the De Soto ran 12th out of a field of 90 cars, 59 of which qualified for the Grand National Event, today called the Sprint Cup. The placement was strong for a finned MoPar with the wrong tires and fresh from a day-long, thousand-mile-plus drive, and with a sleepless driver.

"I had the only new Chrysler in the field," he said. "Chrysler was not sponsoring. All I had was a number — there was not a [sponsor's] sticker on the car. When I came back in the pits, everybody came around me. Fred Lorenzen said, 'That thing really goes!' Lee and Richard Petty and track owner Bill France were among the other stars gathered around the De Soto in the garage area.

Once in the race, the De Soto didn't let him down.

"The [Chrysler Corp.] engines were really good," Hentges said. "You could twist them as far as you could twist, but the ignition would burn out at 6,200 rpm.

"The car handled really well — I attribute that to the fins... [that made it] handle like an arrow.

"It was quite a different feeling driving that car," he said. "The fins didn't make it go faster, but it handled better."

With a field of legends such as Curtis Turner, Fireball Roberts and the Pettys, the competition was hard and the attrition rate was high.

"A lot of engines blew," said Hentges, who had his own problems two-thirds of the way through the race.

"At about 350 miles, I stopped and changed the fan belt and went back out," he said. "It wasn't very long after that when a valve spring retainer broke. It wasn't the car's fault, it was that the valve retainers weren't made for the Isky cam."

Hentges and the De Soto finished 37th out of 59 overall (combined Grand National and convertible class), and 26th among his peers in the Grand National class. He even bested Fireball Roberts, whom he feared would be hard to beat, as well as Buck Baker and Richard Petty, who had been anything but friendly to the Yankee from Minnesota.

Departing with the De Soto

Hentges hung around to see the end of the historic 1959 Daytona 500 race, which defined a true "photo finish."

At the finish line, Lee Petty's 1959 Oldsmobile SceniCoupe and the 1959 Ford Thunderbird coupe driven by Johnny Beauchamp were nose to nose, but Beauchamp immediately appeared to be the winner and was told to drive to victory lane where he was awarded the win. However, photographic evidence at the finish line made the win questionable, and the results were determined unofficial. About 60 hours after the race ended, photographs taken by several photographers at the finish line proved Petty and his Olds took the checkered flag and Beauchamp and his Thunderbird were actually in second.

When it was time to leave, Hentges built a tow bar to tug the De Soto home. Once home, he worked to get the nearly new De Soto running again so it could be sold. The trip had been on a shoestring budget, and there was little, if any, money left to buy a new powerplant. Luckily, a local dealer had the answer.

"I went to Town and Country Motors in St. Paul and talked to a guy and asked if they had any engines they could sell me," Hentges said. "They said they didn't have any they could sell me, but they had a Fireflite engine that kept overheating. He said, 'We can give you that engine since the factory has already written it off.' I could not see anything wrong with it, but when I took the freeze plugs out and saw the casting flashing blocking the coolant flow, I knew what the problem was." With the car running, Hentges said "good-bye."

"That was a tough thing to do," Hentges said. "I really wanted to keep it, but I had a business and didn't have the money to make the payments.

"One guy, a customer, he wanted that car," Hentges said. "He traded me two '56 Fords and $500 cash for [the De Soto]. I sold one and kept the other."

Hentges never drove in another NASCAR race, but he did finish the remainder of the season in a Chrysler at Twin Cities Speedway in Minnesota. After that season in 1959, Hentges did not race again until 1963, which was his last racing season. However, he kept working under the hoods of race-inspired cars.

"I had customers around the Twin Cities who had me tune up their long-ram [manifold] Chrysler engines and put J-2 Oldsmobile engines in Studebaker Golden Hawks for customers" he said.

Today, Hentges operates a small construction firm in California, and although he's given up cylinder heads and carburetors for nails and two-by-fours, his fondness for racing MoPars still rumbles through 50 years later.

CHAPTER 32 | 1959 GENERAL MOTORS
By Phil Hall

'50s FINALE

GM reached for the sky with controversial new designs in '59

The king of fins, the 1959 Cadillac, shows off its towering tail on a six-window Series 62 with a roof design shared only with Buick.

General Motors Corp. has often been accused of moving at the speed of a glacier in making major decisions, but such was not the case when it came to the design of its 1959 model cars.

In late 1956, final touches were being applied to the styling of the 1959 models, and they would continue the Harley Earl-inspired bulky lines of the 1958 models. Chevrolet and Pontiac were to be all-new for 1958, while Oldsmobile, Buick and Cadillac were to be in their second season with shells introduced for 1957.

Evolutionary progression of styling themes was doing quite well for GM at the time. But everything virtually went out the window when the 1957 Chrysler Corp. products with Flightsweep styling were spied. Not only did the MoPars sprout huge Virgil Exner rear fins, but roof lines were low, bodies were long and wide, and glass area was expanded. It was quickly realized that the proposed 1959 GM cars looked like museum pieces in comparison.

An edict went out to start over and emulate the Chrysler designs for every GM

133

Although not the most shocking 1959 GM model, new Buick styling nonetheless caught its typical customer off guard with delta fins and canted headlamps. Top Buicks, such as the Electra 225 pace car shown, received a new 401-cid V-8 that "out-cubed" Cadillac.

brand, and do it now!

In the past, GM used up to three different body shells for its full-sized cars, from A bodies for Chevrolet and Pontiac to B bodies for some Oldsmobiles and Buicks and C bodies for bigger Buicks and Cadillacs. The process varied through the model years.

Condensing the three- to four-year lead times into two meant a need for simplification. Unheard of at GM, one basic body design would have to do for all, from Chevrolet to Cadillac. The choice was a B-body under design at Buick. It was low enough, wide enough and quite in line with visions of the future with large glass area (depending on model). Each division could apply its own design on the front and rear clips, with fins mandatory for the latter.

Meanwhile, in the rest of the domestic auto world, things changed as model year 1959 approached. Chrysler Corp.'s sales boomed for 1957, but quality problems and

Like all 1959 GM models, Oldsmobile was light on the chrome and stainless brightwork. The Oldsmobile with the least amount of trim in '59 was, not surprisingly, the price-leading Dynamic 88, shown here as a Holiday SportSedan (four-door hardtop).

a recession for 1958 left its 1959 models not greatly different from the 1957 models. Ford Motor Co. would ditch the fins on Fords for 1959 and go conservative. American Motors put small fins on 1958 and 1959 standard Ramblers, and Studebaker-Packard had a brief fin fling on 1957-and-later Hawks and all 1958 models, except the Scotsman. For 1959, S-P was pushing its finless compact Lark.

The die was cast when GM introduced its all-new 1959 models. They were shocking to say the least. Each division had its own low, wide grilles and fin designs. The potential drawback of GM standardization of roof designs was hardly noticed. All featured more massive wraparound windshields.

Two-door hardtops featured minimal roof area and plenty of glass. Four-door hardtops (in four-window form) had wraparound rear windows and minimal roof support. There were more conventional six-window, four-door hardtops also available in Buick and Cadillac.

Pillared two- and four-door sedans, available in all but Cadillac, were more conventional with a slightly sloping rear design. Four-door sedans were six-window designs. Station wagons were also unusual with an eight-window configuration, incorporating quarter windows behind the rear doors on four-door models. Tailgates featured re-

Pontiac didn't fear the GM racing promotion ban and openly promoted performance among its models. Pontiacs, such as this Catalina Sport Coupe, could be fitted with 389-cid V-8s that offered up to 345 hp with a NASCAR-breed three-carburetor setup.

tracting windows.

Cadillac Series 75 and Eldorado Brougham were exceptions to the one-body-fits-all program.

Cat's-eye Chevrolets

Chevrolet, advertised as "All New All Over Again," was arguably the most radical of the five with huge cat's-eye tail lamps beneath gull-wing fins and twin vent openings over the low, front grille. Following the theme of the time, it was lower, longer and wider. Wheelbase grew from 117.5 inches to 119, length from 209 inches to 210.9 and width from 77.7 inches to 79.9. All numbers were in great contrast to the now not-so-big 1957 models.

Model lineups changed with Impala no longer a sub-series of the Bel Air. It was now top-of-the-line, adding a four-door sedan and four-door hardtop (Sport Sedan) to the two-door hardtop (Sport Coupe) from 1958. Bel Air was demoted to mid-range and started the year with only two- and four-door sedans. A Sport Sedan was added mid-year. Biscayne received the same degrading, going from the middle slot to entry-level, displacing the Delray.

Wagons continued to have their own designations, but ran parallel to the other

While the front design of the 1959 Chevrolet was contestable, the rear was down-right controversial with a "love it or hate it" look. For the first time, the Bel Air was officially not in the top spot in Chevrolet hierarchy in 1959, though it retained a high-level Sport Sedan (four-door hardtop) model, even as a mid-level Chevrolet.

series. Nomad was at the top, followed by Kingswood and Parkwood in the middle and low-priced Brookwood, which included the only two-door wagon offered by GM that year.

Not a passenger car, but based on one, was the new-for-1959 El Camino pickup, thanks to the Brookwood two-door wagon. It was Chevy's answer to the Ford Ranchero, which bowed mid-year for 1957.

Engine-wise, Chevrolet had the same three basic designs as 1958, with the 235.5-cid Hi-Thrift six, 283 Turbo-Fire V-8 and 348 Turbo Thrust V-8. With GM pledged to not promote performance or racing, development on the 348 was under the guise of law enforcement, and versions up to 320 hp came to market as the model year progressed.

Both Chevrolet and Pontiac utilized the X-frame chassis design they brought out for 1958. It was first seen at GM on the 1957 Cadillacs.

Powerful Pontiacs

Pontiac dealt with the hand it was given for 1959 and did more than any other division to enhance its performance image and sales. The 1959 models were the first fully under the direction of division leader Semon "Bunkie" Knudsen.

Pontiacs featured "Strato-Star Styling," which consisted of split rear fins and a split grille (the first appearance on a production Pontiac of a theme that is used to this day).

Wheelbases remained the same, but series designations were simplified to base Catalina, mid-range Star Chief and top-line Bonneville. As with Chevy, the top-line Bonneville begot a four-door for the first time, the Vista four-door hardtop.

Interestingly, Star Chief did not have a two-door hardtop, but rather the two-door Sport Sedan, while Catalina had both a two-door hardtop and a sedan. Wagons were in the Bonneville and Catalina series and billed as "Safaris."

When it came to attracting attention, the star of the 1959 Pontiac models were "Wide Track Wheels." The front track was some five inches wider this year with the rear not far behind. (Never mind they wouldn't fit on the lifts at many service stations.)

Pontiac went from 370 to 389 cubes for its V-8 and came in versions from 215 to 345 hp. Knudsen openly defied the ban on performance and racing promotion — and got away with it.

Ogle-worthy Oldsmobiles

Meanwhile, over at Oldsmobile, the brand went from king of the chrome in 1958 to a rather clean "Linear Look" 1959 lineup with widely spaced headlamps to rear fins that more resembled twin booms.

Model lineups didn't get shuffled and there was still Dynamic 88, Super 88 and Ninety-Eight series. Chassis-wise, there were not radical changes, and Oldsmobile continued to be the only full-sized GM car with leaf rear springs.

Where creative juices flowed was in body style designations: Two-door hardtops were Holiday SceniCoupes; four-door hardtops were dubbed Holiday SportSedans; and wagons, now all pillared, were called Fiestas.

The 370.7-cid Rocket V-8 from 1958 was reserved for the 1959 Dynamic 88, while a larger Rocket at 394-cid went into the Super 88 and Ninety-Eight versions.

Despite changes, Olds dropped from fourth in sales to sixth for model year 1959.

Buyers back away from Buick

Also falling in popularity was Buick, which slid from fifth to seventh, quite a drop from its third place rank at the middle of the decade. Maybe part of the problem was that Buick, advertised as "The Car," seemingly abandoned its traditional older customers over night. Styling, consisting of the radical delta fins and Ford-like round tail lamps, completely broke with the conservative previous models. Slanted headlamps were above the grille, which held the only link to the 1958 models: Chrome cubes.

While styling was different, it was nothing compared to the model designations. They were completely new, starting with base LeSabre (from a GM dream car), Invicta, Electra and Electra 225 (the latter honoring its overall length).

Buick did offer both four- and six-window four-door hardtops in the Electra 225 line. The style was only shared with Cadillac, as used to be the case when C bodies were used on top-line Buicks.

Engine-wise, Buick, too, pumped up the inches. LeSabres received the previous year's 364-cid V-8, while Invictas and Electras shared the new 401-cid version of the vertical-valve V-8, dubbed the Wildcat 445 for its torque rating.

'Fin king' Cadillacs

If Buick's 1959 moves were controversial, they paled in contrast to the 1959 Cadillac styling. Cadillac takes credit for popularizing the rear fin, starting in 1948, and apparently didn't want to be topped; the 1959 model integrated the largest fins ever on a Cadillac (or any other car, for that matter). Each fin contained two tail lamp spears, just in case the motoring public wasn't paying attention.

Not counting the Series 75, wheelbase was standardized at 130 inches, up from 129.5 the year before, and down from 133 on the previous Series 60 Special.

Eldorado's Seville coupe and Biarritz convertible lost their distinctive rear quarter styling, trading it for revised exterior trim, thanks to the rushing of the 1959 designs into production. Also all-new were the Fleetwood 75 sedan and limousine with formal sedan styling and exclusive 149.75-inch wheelbase.

The Eldorado Brougham was completely redone and now based on the standard Cadillac chassis and inner bodywork, but with four-door hardtop bodies crafted by Pinin Farina in Turin, Italy, and finished in Detroit.

No longer king of the cubic inches at GM, Cadillac upped its V-8 from 365 to 390 for 1959. However, one could still get triple two-barrel carburetors, which were standard on Eldorado two-doors and optional in other selected models.

There is no question that 1959 GM full-sized cars were radical and took the 1957 Chrysler products' styling themes a step or two farther. The question remains: Was it too far? All GM big cars were toned down for 1960, and then downsized and simplified for 1961.

When it came to the fin game, did the 1959 GM cars win, or lose?

Old Cars Report

DATA. PRICING. HISTORY.

Your one-stop resource to provide pricing, data and history on a make and model of your choice.

We've put our fact-filled automotive Standard Catalog of® books plus years of price guide values and auction results into an online, searchable, digital database. Just select a year, make and model—Old Cars Report will compile a report by searching through:

- 25,000 vehicles
- 200,000+ Price Guide values
- 300,000+ auction prices

Each Report includes an image, history, factory info and ID numbers, chassis features, convenience options, current values, historical price trends and related auction prices realized.

The most comprehensive source of automotive content found anywhere.

PRICES STARTING AS LOW AS $4.99

Build your Report now! www.oldcarsreport.com

Old Cars Insider

ONLY $59.98
You save more than $300!

JOIN THE CLUB TODAY!

For almost 40 years, *Old Cars Weekly* has given you reliable pricing, history and news about the classic car industry. Now you can get even MORE automotive expertise when you join our Old Cars Insider Club. It's like a super-sized subscription, designed especially for old car enthusiasts! Here's what you get:

- One-year (52 issues) of *Old Cars Weekly* (retail value: $155.48)*
- One-year access to OldCarsReport.com (retail value: $199.99)
- The exclusive VIP book, '50s Flashback, a decade of classics in pictures (retail value: $12.95)
- Best of Old Cars, a CD compilation from *Old Cars Weekly* (retail value: $9.95)
- 15% off ShopOldCarsWeekly.com purchases for one year
- Plus, exclusive e-newsletters, access to special sales & more!

Join Now at www.oldcarsbookstore.com/club

YOU WILL RECEIVE YOUR OLDCARSREPORT.COM ACCESS INFORMATION VIA EMAIL IN 1-2 BUSINESS DAYS.
THE OLD CARS INSIDER CLUB IS OPEN TO RESIDENTS OF THE UNITED STATES ONLY.
* IF YOU'RE ALREADY A SUBSCRIBER TO *OLD CARS WEEKLY*, YOUR SUBSCRIPTION WILL BE EXTENDED ONE YEAR.

Subscribe to Old Cars
Weekly News & Marketplace
Today!
ONLY 99¢ PER ISSUE

Old Cars Weekly covers the entire field of collectible automobiles—from the classic touring cars and roadsters of the early 1900s, to the popular muscle cars of the 1960s and '70s!

Inside each info-packed issue, you'll get:

- Technical tips and expert restoration advice
- A classified marketplace for cars, parts, and accessories
- Hot news on car shows, swap meets, and auctions
- Personal collectible stories and old car photos
- And much, much more!

Subscribe and save 64% off the cover price!

Act now—subscribe today and get 1 YEAR (56 BIG issues) for just $54.98!

To order online, visit **subscribe.oldcarsweekly.com**

To order by phone, call 386-246-3431—offer J0AHAD

To order by mail, Subscription Processing, P.O. Box 420235, Palm Coast, FL 32142-0235

In Canada, add $90 (includes GST/HST). Outside the U.S. and Canada, add $115. Outside the U.S., remit payment in U.S. funds with order. Please allow 4-6 weeks for first-issue delivery. Annual newsstand rate $155.48. Published weekly.

Get your FREE Muscle Cars Field Guide e-Book!

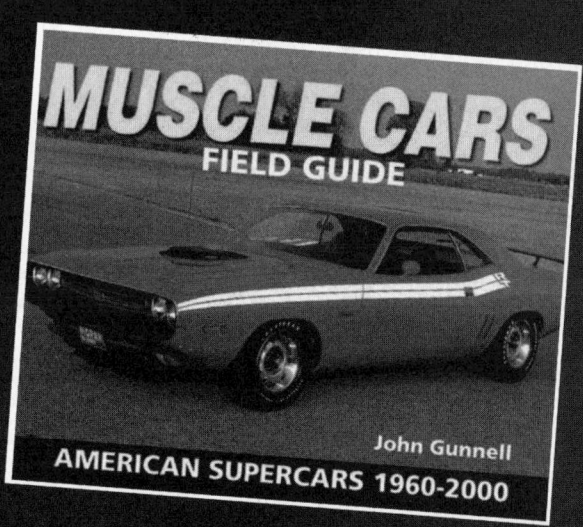

Sign up for yours today!
www.oldcarsweekly.com/Newsletter_Thanks

Note: You must have a valid e-mail address to receive your free e-book

Check out ShopOldCarsWeekly.Com
for Bestselling Car Books, CDs/DVDs, Downloadable Reports, Calendars, Gifts, and More!

Standard Catalog of American Cars
1805-1942, 3rd edition
By Beverly Rae Kimes & Henry Austin Clark, Jr.
Item # AB03 • $74.99

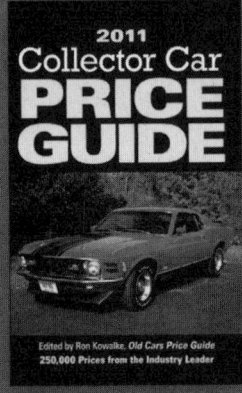

2011 Collector Car Price Guide
By Ron Kowalke
Item # Z7647 • $19.99

Lost & Found
Great Barn Finds & Other Automotive Discoveries
Item # Z8817 • $12.99

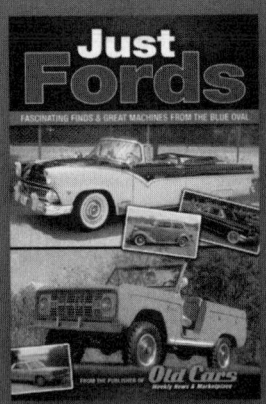

Just Fords
Fascinating Finds & Great Machines From the Blue Oval
Item # Z9996 • $12.99

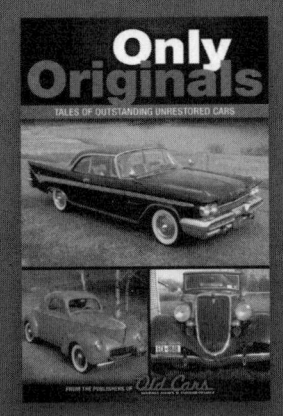

Only Originals
Outstanding Unrestored Cars
Item # Z8818 • $12.99